ook

The Library of Pastoral Care

TITLES ALREADY PUBLISHED

Principles of Pastoral Counselling
R. S. Lee

Casework and Pastoral Care
Jean Heywood

In His Own Parish:
Pastoral Care through Parochial Visiting
Kenneth Child

Understanding the Adolescent
Michael Hare Duke

Marriage Preparation
Martin Parsons

Marriage Counselling
Kenneth Preston

Sick Call: A Book on the
Pastoral Care of the Physically Ill
Kenneth Child

Pastoral Care in Hospitals
Norman Autton

The Pastoral Care of the Elderly
Norman Autton

Pastoral Care and the Drug Scene
Kenneth Leech

Caring for the Elderly
H. T. Storrer

The Pastoral Care of the Dying
Norman Autton

The Pastoral Care of the Bereaved
Norman Autton

IN PREPARATION

The Pastoral Ministry to Children
Anthony Denney

Hearing Confessions
Kenneth N. Ross

God, Man and Pastoral Care
G. R. Dunstan

Other volumes are planned

The Library of Pastoral Care

TITLES ALREADY PUBLISHED

Principles of Pastoral Counselling
R. S. Lee

Casework and Pastoral Care
Jean Heywood

In His Own Parish:
Pastoral Care through Parochial Visiting
Kenneth Child

Understanding the Adolescent
Michael Hare Duke

Marriage Preparation
Martin Parsons

Marriage Counselling
Kenneth Preston

Sick Call: A Book on the
Pastoral Care of the Physically Ill
Kenneth Child

Pastoral Care in Hospitals
Norman Autton

The Pastoral Care of the Mentally Ill
Norman Autton

Pastoral Care and the Drug Scene
Kenneth Leech

Caring for the Elderly
H. P. Steer

The Pastoral Care of the Dying
Norman Autton

The Pastoral Care of the Bereaved
Norman Autton

IN PREPARATION

The Pastoral Ministry to Children
Anthony Denney

Hearing Confessions
Kenneth N. Ross

God, Man, and Pastoral Care
G. B. Austin

Other volumes are planned

PASTORAL CARE AND THE
DRUG SCENE

Pastoral Care and the Drug Scene

KENNETH LEECH
Assistant Curate of St Anne, Soho

LONDON
S · P · C · K
1970

First published in 1970
by S.P.C.K.
Holy Trinity Church
Marylebone Road
London N.W.1

Made and printed in Great Britain by
William Clowes and Sons, Limited
London and Beccles

The two extracts from *Clinical Theology*,
by Frank Lake (Darton, Longman and Todd, 1966)
are used by permission

SBN 281 02470 7

Contents

PREFACE   ix

PART ONE: The Substances Involved in the Drug Scene   1

1. The Emergence of the British Drug Scene   3

2. The Pill Scene   13

3. The Junk Scene   21

4. The "Pot" Scene   37

5. The Acid Scene   49

PART TWO: Pastoral Care in the Drug Scene   57

6. The Social Structure of the Drug Scene   59

7. Pastoral Care and the Drug Scene   80

8. The Spirituality of the Drug Scene   97

9. The Priest and the Drug Scene   116

ABBREVIATIONS   130

NOTES   131

SOME USEFUL ADDRESSES   149

SELECT BIBLIOGRAPHY   153

INDEX   161

Preface

This book is for "straights", that is, for people who do not
belong to the drug scene but wish to understand it, to be
informed about it, and to be of help within it. Those
within the scene should bear this in mind if they read the
book. It is addressed specifically to priests, ministers, and
others whose Christian ministry involves pastoral care of
young people using drugs. I have assumed that accurate
knowledge is indispensable in true pastoral care, and have
therefore devoted Part One to summarizing the data about
drugs which are currently abused. Some readers may find
these chapters hard going, and may prefer to start at
Chapter 6. However, I would advise those involved or likely
to be involved in work on the drug scene to study Part
One. In the past much Christian writing on this subject has
been marked by a conspicuous lack of knowledge. No
genuine pastoral ministry can afford to dispense with the
truth. I therefore make no apology for the use of considerable detail and have included references for almost every
factual assertion.

In Part Two I have drawn, somewhat hesitantly, on
experience in Soho and on the London scene. Work in this
field is relatively new and most of those who are active
within it are, inevitably, in the London area. I have therefore used the London scene as a model in discussing the
nature of pastoral care.

Many people have contributed to whatever value this
book may have. I owe a particular debt of gratitude to my
co-workers in the West End of London, especially to Rod
Moore and Alistair Cox of the Salvation Army Rink Club,
not only for specific information and advice, but also for

their constant support and co-operation on the scene. I am
very grateful to John Wandless, head group pharmacist of
the Woolwich Hospital Group, Don Aitken of the Soma
Research Association, and Mr H. B. Spear of the Home
Office Drugs Branch for checking sections of the manu-
script. The following friends have also helped in various
ways: Steve Abrams, Lisa Biebermann, Major James
Breckenridge, Major Fred Brown, Professor Allan Y.
Cohen, Caroline Coon, The Rev. Henry Cooper, Terence
Deakin, Dr P. T. D'Orban, Rufus Harris, The Rev. J. B.
Harrison, Joseph Havens, Dr I. Pierce James, Dr C. R. B.
Joyce, The Rev. Bill Kirkpatrick, "Doc Livingstone", Kate
and Mike McInnerny, The Rev. Mother Mary Clare,
S.L.G., Father Paulinus Milner, O.P., "Molly", Dom Robert
Petitpierre, O.S.B., Wendy Robson, Chris Simpson, Rheta
Wall, Anton and Marie-Thérèse Wallich-Clifford, and the
Rev. Frank Wilson. I am grateful to the Institute for the
Study of Drug Dependence and the Soma Research Associa-
tion for giving me access to their libraries, to the Church
of England Council for Social Aid for the use of office
facilities, and to Joan de Saumarez-Brock, Mrs Hilda
Loftus, Sandy Spackman, and Marguerite Vaughan for
their help in typing the manuscript.

KENNETH LEECH

10 April 1970

PART ONE

The Substances Involved
in the Drug Scene

First of all I say, as I have often said before, that in the earth are elements of things of every kind: many which serve for food, helpful to life; and many whose property is to cause disease and hasten death. And we have shown before that one thing is more adapted to one, another thing to another living creature for the purposes of life, because of their natures and their textures and their primary elements being all unlike the one to the other. Many which are noxious pass through the ears, many make their way too through the nostrils, dangerous and harsh when they come into contact. And not a few are to be shunned by the touch, and not a few to be avoided by the sight, and others are nauseous in taste.

LUCRETIUS, *De Rerum Natura*

1

The Emergence of the
British Drug Scene

There is no good to be done till the habitual cause is
removed, *viz.* the taking of opium which suddenly to leave
off is (as was shown) very dangerous. Therefore, in order
to leave it off safely, you must stop your hand and not
increase the dose that is taken, by which means it will come
gradually to have little or no effect.... Then only lessen
the 100th part every day till you come to take none at all.

JOHN JONES, 1700[1]

The word "drug" originated by mistake. Arising out of the
Low German *droge vate* ("dry casks"), it was used wrongly
to describe the contents, though the word "drog" simply
meant "dry". Thus, although it is used to describe any
chemical agent affecting live protoplasm, it is, in the strict
sense, not a scientific term.[2] This volume is concerned with
a small number of drugs, those which affect the central
nervous system and, within this limited field, with a certain
number of centrally acting drugs which have been "mis-
used" or "abused". Not all drugs affect the central nervous
system, and not all those which do so have become "drugs
of misuse". To stress this is particularly necessary, since
many people misrepresent drugs as if they were almost evil
in themselves. The drugs with which we are concerned constitute a small proportion of all drugs in use. In Britain
about five thousand drugs, comprising some fifteen hundred
chemical substances, can be prescribed, and about four
hundred of these act on the brain and nervous system.

A drug is defined by the World Health Organization as "any substance that, when taken into the living organism, may modify one or more of its functions".[3] Such a drug may be of vegetable, animal, or mineral origin, or it may be produced synthetically. Many naturally occurring drugs have been used in folk medicine, as well as for pleasure and for religious purposes, for thousands of years. Today the study of drug action and the production of new drugs have become major elements in science. Pharmaceutical chemistry is concerned with the chemical structure of the drug. The study of drug action is called "pharmacology"; the source and characteristics of crude drugs is the concern of "pharmacognosy", while "pharmacy" is the preparation of drugs for medicinal administration.

The precise nature of drug action in many cases is still not clear. The brain is a complex chemical system, and the introduction of drugs into the human organism represents the introduction not of an "artificial" agent into a "natural" creation, but of one biochemical substance into a system of sets of biochemical substances. The relationship between drugs and personality is a two-way one. Different people are affected by a drug in different ways. For instance, some people are stimulated by barbiturates. Drug response is to some extent determined by genetic factors, as well as by dosage, setting, and psychological make-up.

Many drugs, of course, do not affect the central nervous system at all because they cannot enter it from the blood stream. A blood-brain barrier allows only certain types of molecules to enter the brain, although a fever may alter the barrier and enable responses to be made to substances in the bloodstream. "Psycho-chemicals" act upon chemical transmitters within the brain and the effect of a drug is related to the site of its action. The synapses which link the nerve cells release excitatory transmitters (for example, noradrenalin) or inhibitory transmitters (for example, serotonin,) and it is at these points that the drugs act. LSD, for example, seems to block the action of a substance called *serotonin* (5-hydroxytriptamine) in the brain and so throws the serotonergic system temporarily out of order. Similarly chlorpromazine (Largactil) blocks the action of nor-adrenalin.

The drugs with which we are concerned in what is commonly termed "drug abuse" or "drug misuse" fall broadly into four categories. First, hypno-sedatives, which reduce motor activity. Secondly, stimulants, which increase motor activity. Thirdly, "psychedelic" or "psychotomimetic" drugs, which change or widen experience. Fourthly, opiates (opium derivatives) such as morphine and heroin, with analgesic or pain-killing action. These substances must be viewed in the framework of the therapeutic use of drugs, for in one sense "drug abuse" is a side-effect of a revolution in medicine. The central element in this revolution is the use of drugs in the treatment of physical and mental illness.

Before the nineteenth century alcohol and cannabis were widely used for their sedative-hypnotic action. But in 1862 the barbiturates were isolated by Alfred Bayer who named them "Barbara's urates", probably because he made his discovery on 4 December, St Barbara's Day. The first barbiturate to be developed was barbitone, which was not used clinically until 1903. Phenobarbitone was synthesized in 1912, amylobarbitone in 1923, pentobarbitone and quinalbarbitone in 1930. In the 1950s the tranquillizers began to appear. Chlorpromazine was synthesized in Paris in 1950, and marketed as Largactil by May and Baker in 1952. Also in 1950 research on a muscle relaxant led to the discovery of meprobamate. Three years before, chlordiazepoxide (Librium) had been synthesized and this was the first of a series of compounds called benzodiazepines. Diazepam (Valium) and nitrazepam (Mogadon) came into medicinal use in 1960. The same period saw the emergence of anti-depressants such as imipramine (Tofranil) and amitriptyline (Tryptizol), which appeared in 1958 and 1959.[4]

The late 1950s also saw the beginning of a new pattern

of illicit drug use among adolescents, and it is necessary now to clarify the concepts of "drug abuse" and "drug misuse" and to remove from them the inverted commas. I shall define drug misuse as the intermittent misapplication of a drug or drugs, and drug abuse as the continuous misapplication. The drug misuser uses the drug wrongly, perhaps mistakenly; the drug abuser puts it to a bad use.[5] The misuse of some drugs brings about drug dependence, and it is evident that both the major tranquillizers (phenothiazines) and the minor tranquillizers can produce dependence.[6] So far there has been little evidence of a chronic abuse pattern with an illicit market in tranquillizers or anti-depressants, though they figure in adolescent drug scenes from time to time in conjunction with other drugs. Rather, the pattern here is of therapeutic use accompanied on occasions by unpleasant side effects and sometimes by dependence.[7]

What is drug dependence? The World Health Organization's definition is as follows:[8]

> Drug dependence is a state of psychic or physical dependence, or both, on a drug, arising in a person following administration of that drug on a periodic or continuous basis. The characteristics of such a state will vary with the agent involved, and these characteristics must always be made clear by designating the particular type of drug dependence in each specific case: for example, drug dependence of morphine type, or barbiturate type, etc.

This definition of 1964 superseded earlier official terminology which attempted to distinguish "addiction" from "habituation". It was pointed out that drug addiction led to a compulsion to obtain the drug, a tendency to increase the dose, a psychological and usually physical dependence, and detrimental effect on the individual and society: while (it was claimed) habituation did not show a compulsion but only a desire, did not show a tendency to increase the dose, showed no physical dependence or abstinence syndrome, and showed detrimental effects (if any) primarily on the individual. But clearly there were forms of severe psychological dependence which affected society adversely, and there were many variations of drug abuse which made these distinctions highly artificial. A World Health Organization study in 1964 pointed out that individuals may become dependent on a wide variety of chemical substances.[9]

Moreover the use of the words "addiction", "addict", and "addictive" tends to portray the issue in static terms, as if "addiction" were a property of a drug, a kind of pharmacological Thomism. One needs to bring into play a number of forces, pharmacological, psychological, and social, in order to understand the drug dependent state.[10] For drug dependence is the creation of a relationship between a particular personality and a drug of choice within the context of a particular social situation. In Britain until recently there have been two prevalent traditions of drug dependence, one of dependence on opiates, principally morphine and heroin, and the other of dependence on barbiturates. Both of these have been "therapeutic addictions", that is, addictions brought about during medical treatment, or through professional proximity to drugs. Both the opiates and the barbiturates produce an "abstinence syndrome", that is, physical pain and sickness when the drug is withdrawn. The history of these distinct traditions within Britain brings us to the point at which the current scene rests.

1. THE THERAPEUTIC OPIATE ADDICT

> Forty years ago there were no morphinomaniacs, only opium eaters. . . . Nowadays, the syringe of Pravaz is to be found everywhere.   TANZI, 1909[11]

According to legend, the opium poppy grew on the spot where Buddha's eyelids fell when he cut them off to prevent himself from falling asleep. In fact, it had been mentioned long before this in Sumerian tablets of 3000–4000 B.C. Hesiod in the eighth century B.C. refers to a town called Mekone, "the town of the poppy", near Corinth, and both

Herodotus and Hippocrates were aware of the therapeutic value of opium. It has been suggested that opium was introduced to India in the eighth century,[12] but it could have happened a thousand years before.

Illicit use of opium on a significant scale seems to have developed in the late seventeenth century. During the seventeenth century in Britain, Thomas Sydenham prepared laudanum, and "Dover's Powder" was prepared a short time after. John Jones in 1700 described a gradual withdrawal treatment for opium addiction. The first Opium War (1839–42) marked the beginning of the spread of opium addiction in China, and in 1906 an imperial edict forbade the growth of the poppy and the use of opium. In 1909 the International Opium Convention met at Shanghai.

In the meantime morphine, a natural alkaloid of opium, had been extracted in 1830, to be followed shortly by codeine, which later became an essential part of most cough mixtures. Also in the nineteenth century the hypodermic syringe was invented by Pravaz. The literature on morphine dates from 1864, and in 1875 Levinstein first used the word "euphoria", as a description of the state of well-being induced by morphine. In 1886 Erlenmeyer referred to the danger of "cocomania", the combination of morphine and cocaine which was to play so important a role in the subsequent history of addiction.[13]

Cocaine had been the first local anaesthetic used in medicine. It had been isolated by Albert Niemann in 1857 from coca brought from Peru. Legend describes the origin of the coca leaf in the Andes, after the Yungas were exiled there by Khunu, the God of Thunder. The misuse of coca is far more common throughout the world than that of cocaine. In Britain there has been little incidence of the misuse of cocaine alone since the mid-1920s. In the nineteenth century, while the use of morphine and cocaine grew, the working classes were more likely to use laudanum.

The 1909 Shanghai Conference was followed in 1912 by the Hague Opium Convention which recommended international control, and the Harrison Act 1914 in the United States and the Dangerous Drugs Act 1920 in the United Kingdom were the direct results of this convention. In 1926 the Departmental Committee on Morphine and Heroin Addiction (the Rolleston Committee) produced its Report which laid down the principles on which the so-called "British system" of treatment of addicts has been based: that the addict was to be treated as a sick person, and that the prescribing of the necessary amount of the drug for proper functioning ("maintenance dosage") was a legitimate exercise of medical responsibility. By the 1930s opiate addiction in Britain seemed to be under control. Between 1935 and 1953 the total number of addicts declined from 700 to 290: they were mainly middle-aged and were addicted either to morphine or to synthetic analgesics such as pethidine. Indeed, as late as 1967, 36 per cent of women addicts were aged over fifty and only 8 per cent of these were using heroin. It was only in 1963 that male addicts exceeded female.[14] Until the mid-fifties, the picture of opiate addiction in Britain was one of a small and decreasing group of therapeutic (and "professional"), middle-aged and elderly morphine addicts, widely dispersed geographically, and rarely in contact with one another. Confidently, the British Government reported to the United Nations in 1955: "Addiction is not a serious problem in the United Kingdom."[15]

2. THE BARBITURATE ADDICT

> But the night is long
> and I am full of tossing till the dawn. *Job 7.4*

Chloral hydrate, discovered in 1869, and paraldehyde, discovered in 1882, historically followed the discovery of the barbiturates, but they came into medicinal use first. Until 1903, when barbitone (Veronal) was introduced, chloral hydrate and paraldehyde were the most widely used hypnotics. But from 1903 the barbiturates quickly became popular, and this popularity has not significantly declined with the development of "non-barbiturate hypnotics". The first case of chronic abuse of barbiturates was recorded in 1904 by R. Laudenheimer. In 1906 the Registrar-General reported the first case of fatal barbiturate poisoning, and in 1908 the first two suicides.

Between 1911 and the present day there has occurred a serious increase in deaths from barbiturates. In 1962, of all deaths over the age of 15 in England and Wales, barbiturates killed 1 in 441 men and about 1 in 306 women.[16] The danger of physical dependence was noted in 1934[17] and in 1946 it was estimated that enough barbiturates were being produced in Britain to provide "one sleeping tablet per head per day for a million of the population".[18]

The barbiturate drugs depress the central nervous system, and they fall into four categories:

1. *Long-acting*, for example, phenobarbitone. The action begins after one hour and lasts 8–10 hours. It is used in the treatment of epilepsy.
2. *Intermediate-acting*, for example, butobarbitone (Soneryl), pentobarbitone (Nembutal), amylobarbitone (Amytal). The action begins in half an hour and lasts about 6 hours. They are used in the treatment of insomnia.
3. *Short-acting*, for example, quinalbarbitone (Seconal). The action begins in fifteen minutes and lasts 2–3 hours. They are used for those with ordinary difficulties in sleeping.
4. *Ultra-short-acting*, for example, thiopentone sodium (Pentothal), hexobarbitone sodium (Brietal). These are used as anaesthetics given intravenously.[19]

G. B. Adams, who studied an urban general practice in London, reported that 407 patients out of a practice of 10,000 were receiving barbiturates. They were mainly women aged 49–54.[20] An earlier study analysed all prescriptions for barbiturates issued in February and March 1959: 31 per cent were for phenobarbitone, 20 for Amytal,

14 for Soneryl, 10 for Drinamyl, 6 for Nembutal, and 19 for other forms.[21] By 1965, the annual number of prescriptions for barbiturates in the United Kingdom was seventeen million. Between 1956 and 1965, suicides from barbiturates rose from 515 to 1490, and accidental deaths from 140 to 525.

The barbiturates produce a withdrawal syndrome which varies with the dose. Anxiety, headache, nervousness, tremor, and vomiting after eight hours may become more intense and severe up to a period of a day, after which convulsions may take place. In the relief of barbiturate withdrawal, the phenothiazines have been found sometimes to precipitate convulsions while milder tranquillizers have proved impotent.[22] The usual method is to give 200–400 mg. of pentobarbitone sodium, and reduce the dose by ten per cent over a ten day period.

Barbiturate dependence has been described as "the worst possible form of addiction, unsightly, deteriorating, difficult to treat".[23] There are several types of barbiturate abuse (apart from the abuse by heroin addicts which will be discussed later). The most common type is the patient who seeks sedation, almost to the point of oblivion. The elderly person who simply cannot sleep represents the typical barbiturate user, and some degree of dependence seems common among this group. A different type of addict is the person who wants the excitement of intoxication following tolerance, a pattern similar to alcoholic abuse. The "cyclical" abuser will combine abuse of barbiturates for sedation with abuse of amphetamines for stimulation. Desk workers under heavy pressure, entertainers, and night-life fiends are obvious examples of this type. More recently barbiturate abuse has spread to the adolescent illicit market.

The development of "non-barbiturate hypnotics" such as glutethimide (Doriden), methylprylone (Nodular), methaqualone (Melsed, Mondrax), and nitrazepam (Mogadon) has opened up a new area for abuse of barbiturate-type among adolescents. But the problem of dependence of barbiturate type remains predominantly among adult patients, and studies have expressed concern at the danger of abuse of the newer hypnotics.[24] It is among adult patients also that the dangers of abuse of amphetamine (prescribed for therapeutic purpose), anti-depressants and tranquillizers chiefly lie. And, in numerical terms, as well as in terms of destructive potential, the most disturbing feature of this picture is that, if Adams's figures are in any sense representative of the country as a whole, "approximately two million people in Great Britain are receiving barbiturates at any one time and 80 per cent of the total are female".[25] It is against this background of "therapeutic addiction" and of a society geared to the use of tablets that the emerging adolescent "pill scene" of the 1950s must be seen.

2

The Pill Scene

1. THE SPREAD OF THE AMPHETAMINES

The drugs of this group have the advantage of being relatively non-toxic, addiction to them is rare, and there are no
serious ill effects; they may therefore be given to out-patients
without undue risk.   *Ministry of Health Report*, 1955[1]

The production of Drinamyl by Smith, Kline, and French
in 1951 in the form of a "purple heart" may be seen as the
event which ushered in the "pep pill" era. In fact, Drinamyl
was neither purple nor heart-shaped, but blue and tri-
angular, and when in 1964 the shape became round, it
became known by the simpler name of "blues". Drinamyl
combined dexamphetamine and amylobarbitone and was
found to be useful in a variety of conditions. It was common as an anti-fatigue and slimming agent for some years
before "purple hearts" entered the adolescent drug scene.
Moreover, Drinamyl came at the end of a long period of
work on the amphetamines.

Amphetamine was first prepared in 1887 by Edeleano,
and methylamphetamine in 1919 by Ogata in Japan. The
first important pharmacological studies were made by
Alles in 1927.[2] In 1932 amphetamine was introduced as a
nasal decongestant in the form of the Benzedrine inhaler.
It was used for the treatment of narcolepsy in 1935, and of
depression in 1936. Methylamphetamine, known in Germany under the trade name Pervitin, was found to be
specially useful for the treatment of apathetic and depressed
psychopathic conditions. Methylamphetamine injection

was used first as a vasopressor agent in surgical emergencies, and this has remained its main use. Amphetamine (Benzedrine) was soon split into dextro-and laevo-rotatory forms, rotating polarized light to right or left. Dexamphetamine (Dexedrine) is approximately twice as potent as a stimulant as amphetamine. The amphetamine drugs are stimulants of the central nervous system. The word "sympathomimetic" was first used of them in 1910, and this action appears to originate in the hypothalamus.

As early as 1938 it was realized that misuse of amphetamine could bring about a psychotic condition, and the first description of such a mental state was by Young and Scoville in the United States.[3] In 1947 there were further reports from the United States of psychoses in young prisoners who had swallowed the contents of Benzedrine inhalers.[4] There were similar reports of methylamphetamine psychoses, the first detailed description coming from Germany in 1941. The similarities to the effects of cocaine were striking. But it was Japan which provided the most disturbing evidence of the serious mental hazards of amphetamine abuse. The Japanese epidemics after 1948, and particularly in 1954, were estimated to have affected about half a million users.[5] Chronic psychoses were recorded in 14 per cent of 492 Japanese methylamphetamine users in a study in 1963, which also claimed that the effect could last as long as 15 years.[6] Another serious epidemic occurred in Sweden, beginning in the 1940s, and this also involved the use of another amphetamine-like substance phenmetrazine (Preludin).[7]

The beginnings of amphetamine abuse among young people in Britain are not clearly documented. Attention was not focussed on the dangers of such abuse in medical literature much before 1958, and concern did not express itself in the popular press until 1963. But by the early 1950s there was some abuse of Dexedrine and of Drinamyl, certainly among students by 1952 and in the emerging coffee bar and club clientele in Soho shortly afterwards. It was Dr P. H. Connell who described "amphetamine psychosis" at length in the British literature,[8] and subsequent papers have repeated, rather than added to, his observations. Connell himself has continued to contribute papers on amphetamine abuse, but they do not add significantly to the information available in his early papers.[9] Recently, the British Medical Association's Working Party on Amphetamine Preparations has concluded that, with the exception of their use in narcolepsy, there seems little justification for the continued use of these drugs.[10] Nevertheless, the illicit market continues, little, if any, of it fed by illicit manufactures.

In Britain the drugs of this group most commonly used are: (i) *Dexedrine*: yellow tablets. (ii) *Dexedrine Spansules*: capsules, brown and speckled white and orange. (iii) *Daprisal*: tablets containing amphetamine and amylobarbitone oblong, faintly yellow. (iv) *Dexten*: Dexamphetamine tablets, yellow, plain, and round. (v) *Dexytal*: amphetamine and amylobarbitone sodium, pink capsules. (vi) *Durophet*: amphetamine capsules: 12·5 mg. black and white; 20 mg. black. (vii) *Durophet-M*: amphetamine and methaqualone, capsules: 12·5 mg. brown and green; 20 mg. brown and red. (viii) *Drinamyl*: Dexamphetamine and amylobarbitone, tablets, blue. (ix) *Drinamyl Spansules*: Dexamphetamine and amylobarbitone, green capsules with green and white pellets, two strengths. (x) *Methedrine*: methylamphetamine hydrochloride: tablets, white, 5 mg.; ampoules (injectable) 30 mg.

Methylamphetamine is found in combination with pentobarbitone in *Desbutal* capsules and with phenobarbitone in *Diesed* tablets, and in sustained action tablets in *Metamsustac*.[11] The supply of injectible methylamphetamine has been restricted to hospitals since October 1968, and tablets too have ceased to play a significant part in the drug market. Similar in action to the amphetamines are phenmetrazine (Preludin), phentermine (Duromine), mephentermine (Mephine), and methylphenidate (Ritalin).

Amphetamines have been used in a wide range of conditions. Their use in the treatment of depression is certainly obsolete[12] and it is probable that this also applies to the treatment of certain behaviour problems in children, epilepsy, aggressive psychopathy, enuresis, menstrual problems, fatigue, and poisoning from barbiturates. In the treatment of narcolepsy their value is generally recognized, although there have been claims that methylphenidate is more effective.[13] The use of methylamphetamine for abreaction in psychiatry is not widespread, but it is still used in anaesthesia, for restoration of blood pressure. In general practice the prescribing of amphetamine preparations is mainly for obesity, depression, tiredness, and anxiety.[14]

Concern about the misuse of amphetamines has centred around two points. The first is the danger of psychological dependence which various writers have referred to as "amphetamine addiction".[15] The second is the undoubted fact that in large doses these drugs can bring about a psychotic condition. Connell claimed in 1958,[16]

> The psychotic picture is identical with paranoid schizophrenia but, without a lengthy follow-up with biochemical control, only speculation is possible.

The condition is characterized by paranoid delusions and vivid hallucinations of all the senses. There may be confusion and violent excitement. Psychoses usually develop after daily doses of 100 to 500 mg. but there have been reports of psychoses after only 50 mg. while many people have used up to 500 mg. per day without becoming psychotic.[17] In a study of 74 regular young methylamphetamine users in London in 1968, 82 per cent were found to have delusions of persecution or ideas of reference, 54 per cent had visual hallucinations, 59 per cent auditory hallucinations, and 59 per cent tactile hallucinations. 24 per cent reported "bugs", a common feature of methylamphetamine use, and 50 per cent reported thought disorder.[18] The psychosis is most powerful in the use of methylamphetamine and it has been claimed that permanent organic brain damage may occur.[19]

Between 1960 and 1966 the pill scene was a fairly conservative one, involving a small number of proprietary manufactures. The adolescent amphetamine users fell into two categories, the sporadic "weekender" type who used Drinamyl as a "wakeamine" in the context of all-night club sessions, and the chronic "pillhead" type for whom the pill scene was a way of life. Both types were involved in a pattern of *oral* drug use and there was little contact between these pill-taking communities and the heroin addict groups. It was in 1966 that injectible methylamphetamine began to appear and its use reached a peak in 1968. The spread of Methedrine ampoules into the pill scene brought together the heroin addict and the pillhead and created also a new type of intravenous drug user—the "meth freak". Moreover the sources of supply pointed to a very small group of general practitioners, and it was difficult to see on what clinical arguments their practice of "Methedrine maintenance" could be justified.[20]

By 1968 the use of Methedrine had become a subcultural activity in which the ritual of injection played a major role. When in October 1968 the Ministry of Health reached an agreement with the manufacturers to restrict the supplies of injectible methylamphetamine for one year to hospitals, there was an immediate search for injectible substitutes. For a short time methylphenidate (Ritalin) became the popular alternative to Methedrine. This drug had been available in Britain since 1955 and its use had never been great. The manufacturers became worried when their sales figures for January 1967 to August 1968 showed that, while sales of tablets had changed very little, sales of ampoules had shown a major increase. Commendable action by the manufacturer brought this mini-epidemic to an end in mid-October 1968,[21] and, although there have been occasional reports of abuse and psychosis elsewhere,[22] the drug has played a negligible role in the British scene. Similarly, although the abuse of phenmetrazine (Preludin) in Sweden has led to serious casualties with numerous reports of dependence and psychosis,[23] this drug has not figured very prominently in the British adolescent pill market.

By the end of 1968 there was a very disturbed subcultural group within London for whom the process of injection was more important than the substance injected. The fact that a number of former Methedrine users subsequently changed to intravenous use of methadone (Physeptone), heroin, or barbiturates, drugs with quite opposite effects, suggests that "any theory which seeks to relate specific drug choice to personality or to a particular type of reaction against society is simple-minded".[24] Nevertheless, over the country as a whole, it is oral use of amphetamines which has prevailed, and even in London the majority of young drug abusers act within a fairly restricted conventional framework. However, a recent disturbing development has been the entry into the pill scene of barbiturates and of "non-barbiturate hypnotics".

2. THE ENTRY OF "SLEEPERS" INTO THE PILL SCENE

They reel to and fro, and stagger like
a drunken man: and are at their wit's end
Psalm 107.27

In the last chapter, the similarity between barbiturate and alcoholic intoxication was noted, and it is the intoxicant effect which is so important in the adolescent scene. The early abusers of hypnotics of the barbiturate type were, as was shown, of therapeutic origin and, on the whole, middle-aged and elderly. The entry of "sleepers" (hypnotic drugs) into the adolescent pill scene came about by two routes. The first was through the use of barbiturates by heroin addicts. In almost every case the drug of choice is Tuinal, a red and blue capsule which contains equal parts of amylobarbitone and quinalbarbitone. The addict uses the barbiturate to potentiate the effect of heroin, thus achieving a state of peace followed by near-oblivion. The recent reduction in the amount of heroin prescribed, and therefore in the amount available on the illicit market, has led to increased use of barbiturates by injection. In the United States barbiturates and other hypnotics play a major part in the adolescent scene. Thus one American writer has claimed that "glutethimide . . . has achieved . . . a large position in the life of the adolescent drug addict", that it is "second only to heroin in desirability by the addict" and "is sold on the street for from 50 cents to $1 a pill".[25] What is new in Britain is the *intravenous* use of barbiturates on a significant scale by both heroin addicts and others.

The second route by which "sleepers" became popular was through the increased availability of the "non-barbiturate hypnotics" among a widely dispersed section of the adolescent population. By 1961, 2·5 to 3 per cent of National Health Service prescriptions in England and Wales were for non-barbiturate hypnotics and sedatives.[26] Their use among adolescents, however, did not become widespread until after 1966. Moreover, while in the United States it had been glutethimide (Doriden) which had caused concern,[27] in Britain the anxiety was to focus upon a drug called Mandrax, which during 1968 attained an ominous popularity among heroin addicts[28] and also spread throughout other sections of the drug-taking population.

Mandrax, produced by Roussel Laboratories, contains methaqualone combined with an antihistamine, diphenhydramine. The recommended dose is one tablet. Methaqualone had earlier been marketed by Boots under the name Melsedin, and is contained in Riker's Durophet-M capsules. Mandrax acts upon the reticular formation of the brain stem and action begins in 15 to 30 minutes, producing a hypnotic effect lasting 6 to 8 hours. Its action is much more selective than that of the barbiturates, and it therefore was found to be a valuable hypnotic with less likelihood of dependence than was the case with barbiturates.[29] However, a combination of Mandrax with alcohol was found to produce prolonged heavy sedation, and there have been cases of alleged hallucinogenic effects from this combination. In addition methaqualone potentiates the effect of codeine, methadone, and some tranquillizers. The dangers of abuse of methadone (Physeptone) and methaqualone (Mandrax) were noted in a report from a clinic in Chelsea in 1969[30] and it has been pointed out that a combination of chlorpromazine (Largactil) with Mandrax could be "a particularly lethal combination".[31]

Soon after the introduction of Mandrax in 1965, cases of poisoning were reported. During the seven months following its appearance, 5 per cent of poisoned persons admitted to the Poisoning Treatment Centre at Edinburgh Royal Infirmary were suffering from Mandrax overdose.[32] Cases of overdose with 20, 30, 40, and even 60 tablets did not prove to be fatal[33] though one case of death was reported from 30 tablets.[34] Mandrax overdose shows a characteristic pattern with marked hypermotor activity and sometimes severe convulsions. The patient may be unconscious for hours or days. Intensive supportive therapy is the best treatment, and experts advise strongly against forced diuresis or attempts to hasten the removal of Mandrax from the body.[35]

The effect of hypnotics is exactly opposed to that of stimulants. The amphetamine abuser will be highly excited, restless, possibly violent, irritable, and over-sensitive; the hypnotic abuser will be confused, unco-ordinated in speech and movement, drowsy, and will stumble around in a drunken stupor. Both types of effect are desired and produced within a pill scene which is increasingly one of multiple drug abuse.

3

The Junk Scene

1. THE PATTERN OF HEROIN ADDICTION IN BRITAIN

> After careful consideration of all the data put before us we are of the opinion that in Great Britain the incidence of addiction to dangerous drugs...is still very small.... There is nevertheless in our opinion no cause to fear that any real increase is at present occurring.
>
> *Drug Addiction Report of the*
> *Interdepartmental Committee 1961*[1]

Between 1935 and 1953 the number of addicts known to the Home Office fell from around 700 to 290. From 1954 the number began to rise. In 1958 there were 442, of whom 62 were using heroin, and this rose to 454 in 1959, of whom 68 were using heroin. In 1960 there was a drop in the total figure to 437 but an increase in the number using heroin to 94. Unlike the earlier addicts, who were mainly middle-aged or elderly morphine addicts, the new addicts were aged between 15 and 35, and their addiction was non-

	1959	1960	1961	1962	1963	1964	1965	1966	1967	1968
Using heroin	68	94	132	175	237	342	521	899	1299	2240
Male	196	195	223	262	339	490	558	886	1262	2161
Female	258	242	247	270	296	344	369	463	467	621
TOTAL	454	437	470	532	635	753	927	1349	1729	2782

TABLE 1. Drug Addicts Known to the Home Office 1959–68

therapeutic in origin. Table 1 shows the increase between 1959 and 1968.

Before 1960, there were no addicts under 20, but the first one appeared in that year, and Table 2 shows the subsequent increase:

Year	Number
1959	—
1960	1
1961	2
1962	3
1963	17
1964	40
1965	145
1966	329
1967	395
1968	764

TABLE 2. Drug Addicts Known to the Home Office 1959–68
Under the Age of 20

Almost all these new addicts began to use heroin illicitly. Between 1954 and 1964 there were only 14 new cases of therapeutic addiction, contrasted with 436 of non-therapeutic origin. James[2] estimated the proportion of heroin addicts per million of the population in the respective age groups in 1966 to be as follows: 15–19: 75·9; 20–34: 47·5; 35–49: 8·1; 49 and over: 1·2. Thus in Britain in 1966 the proportion of heroin addicts was 22·1 per million of the population.

The spectacular increase in 1966 continued in 1967. In that year the number of heroin addicts rose from 899 to 1299, an increase of 44 per cent. The youngest addicts in that year were 3 aged 15, 38 aged 16, 82 aged 17, and 100 aged 18.[3] By the following year, the year in which compulsory notification was introduced, there had been a net increase of addicts of all dangerous drugs (that is, drugs controlled under the Dangerous Drugs Act) of 1053 (61 per cent). Heroin addicts rose from 1299 to 2240, an increase of 72 per cent. There was an increase in the numbers of addicts under the age of 20 from 395 to 764 (93 per cent) of whom 709 were using heroin. Ten were aged 15, and the peak age of heroin addicts was 20. In 1968, 79 per cent of all addicts were under the age of 25.[4] Table 3 shows the age structure of addicts in 1968:

AGE	Male		Female		Total	
	All Drugs	Heroin	All Drugs	Heroin	All Drugs	Heroin
Under 15	—	—	—	—	—	—
15	6	6	4	4	10	10
16	37	34	3	3	40	37
17	122	116	19	16	141	132
18	228	207	46	44	274	251
19	247	235	52	44	299	279
20	295	280	53	52	348	332
21	246	231	38	36	284	267
22	199	181	41	39	240	220
23	113	99	26	24	139	123
24	99	89	23	21	122	110
25	65	61	24	23	89	84
26	47	42	19	16	66	58
27	53	43	13	10	66	53
28	36	30	6	6	42	36
29	28	23	7	5	35	28
30	22	16	8	6	30	22
31	25	22	4	2	29	24
32	15	13	3	3	18	16
33	10	9	3	2	13	11
34	8	5	1	1	9	6
35–49	108	63	38	15	146	78
50 and over	94	7	166	13	260	20
Unknown	58	35	24	8	82	43
TOTAL	2161	1847	621	393	2782	2240

TABLE 3. Classification of Addicts according to Age and Sex 1968

3

The "marked increase in the number of persons addicted to diacetylmorphine [heroin], especially in the younger age groups", was first noted in the Government's Report to the United Nations for 1964.[5] In that year the Interdepartmental Committee on Drug Addiction under Lord Brain, which in 1961 had reported that the incidence of addiction was very small and that there was no indication of an increase, was reconvened to consider the position and make recommendations. Its Report was published in 1965.[6] In that year, there was a further increase in heroin addiction, the new cases being almost entirely confined to young people. There was a "significant increase in the number of addicts who have obtained their drugs entirely from unknown sources":[7] this number had risen from 5 in 1964 to 77 in 1965. There was at this stage little evidence of traffic in heroin which was fed entirely from illicit sources.[8] By 1967 the Home Office found it impossible to distinguish between addicts who had obtained their drugs from licit sources by illicit means and those who had used illicit sources entirely, but it was believed that 306 addicts (including the "unknown sources") fell into this category.[9]

The Brain Report of 1965 pointed out that the major source of supply of heroin had been a small group of doctors who had prescribed very large amounts, and six doctors in London were specifically mentioned.[10] In fact there was never a static group of doctors (the number rarely falling below six or rising above twelve) who prescribed for significant numbers of addicts. The doctors were not the same for any one period, and some of the most appalling instances of irresponsible prescribing began to occur after the Brain Report. The "junkies' doctors" fell into three categories: first, those who attempted treatment and therapy on an out-patient basis or in liaison with a hospital or nursing home; secondly, those who simply "maintained" the addict, with little hope of "curing" him, but out of sheer humanity; and, thirdly, those who exploited and aggravated the situation by massive over-prescribing without any real attempt to help. The blanket condemnation of these doctors, often by persons with only a remote contact with drug addiction, has been regrettable. Some of them were dedicated, humane physicians who for years attempted to help a section of the population whom most of their colleagues would not touch, and they carried out their lonely task without support or help from medical official-dom. It is possible that if more doctors had involved them-selves in the scene at an early stage the development of the British heroin problem would have been different.

The Brain Report recommended that only licensed doctors should be able to prescribe heroin and cocaine for addicts, and that they should be compelled to notify all such addicts to the central authority. Most of the recom-mendations of the Report were embodied in the Dangerous Drugs Act 1967 and the regulations which followed it. The Act also empowered the police, from 27 October 1967, to search persons and vehicles where there were "reasonable grounds" to suspect unauthorized possession of drugs, extended police powers of arrest in regard to suspected narcotic drug offences, and substituted ten years for two years as the maximum sentence for an offence under the Customs and Excise Act 1952 relating to narcotic drugs. The Dangerous Drugs (Notification of Addicts) Regulations 1968 came into operation on 22 February 1968, and required doctors who attended a person whom they considered or reasonably suspected to be an addict of a dangerous drug to notify the Chief Medical Officer of the Home Office. The Dangerous Drugs (Supply to Addicts) Regulations 1968, which came into operation on 16 April 1968, prohibited doctors not licensed by the Secretary of State from prescrib-ing heroin and cocaine for addicts. At the same time the long awaited "treatment centres" began to appear.

One of the fears expressed by those within the drug scene was that the disappearance of the "junkies' doctors" might lead to the expansion of the illicit market in heroin. There was talk of the Mafia "moving in", and Britain "going the

New York way". Certainly the appearance of the treatment
centres has led to a reduction in the amount of heroin
prescribed, although there are variations from one clinic
to another. Thus between August 1968 and March 1969
the total amount of heroin prescribed by the treatment
centres fell by over 20 per cent.[11] But, it seemed, the most
likely result was not an epidemic of imported heroin but
rather a search for injectible substitutes. Thus a treatment
centre doctor warned that "a group of young Physeptone
addicts is emerging".[12] Physeptone (methadone hydrochloride), the synthetic analgesic drug used in heroin withdrawal, was itself becoming a major problem in 1968, and
the addicts involved included a large number who had
never been hardened heroin addicts but had progressed to
injectible Physeptone from the amphetamines.

Nevertheless, there has been an increase in illicit imported heroin. Known as "Chinese", the circulation of
brown powder, allegedly from Hong Kong, began in Soho,
and it is Soho which has remained the major source of
supply. Heroin is easily made in Hong Kong, where it is
smoked rather than injected and is generally of poor
quality. Many Hong Kong addicts use barbiturate as a base
powder, and the combination of heroin and barbiturate
("red chicken") has increased there over the last eight
years.[13] An article in an English newspaper[14] sparked off a
series of reports, most of them virtually identical, about the
epidemic of Chinese heroin in Soho. The main difficulty
with powder heroin is that one cannot guarantee the dosage
or the purity, and so overdose and poisoning are likely.
The mixing of heroin with strychnine and poisonous substances has been reported frequently, and the sale of talcum
powder, crushed "Oxo" cubes, curry powder, and even
"Horlicks" to naive experimenters is not unknown. So far
the traffic in powder heroin has not spread on a significant
scale beyond London.

The geographical concentration of heroin addicts within
London has been a feature of the scene since its early days.

Many of the present "hard core" addicts can be traced back, by person-to-person infection, to a group of West End addicts in the early 1950s A less important role was also played by a group of around seventy Canadian addicts who left Canada between 1959 and 1962, though around half of these had died or returned by the end of 1965. Almost all the new addicts who were emerging were within London, although there were no "addict neighbourhoods" within London. The number of heroin addicts receiving

Area	In Patient	Out Patient
London	87	798
Metropolitan Areas: N.W.	13	7
„ „ N.E.	—	—
„ „ S.E.	6	13
„ „ S.W.	13	18
Newcastle	—	—
Leeds	7	12
Sheffield	3	2
East Anglia	1	21
Oxford	3	5
South-West	1	—
Wales	—	—
Birmingham	6	29
Manchester	2	3
Liverpool	4	13
Wessex	5	24
Scotland	1	5
TOTAL OUTSIDE LONDON	65	152

TABLE 4. Heroin Addicts Receiving Treatment on 31 May 1968[15]

treatment as in-patients or out-patients throughout the country on 31 May 1968 (Table 4) shows that the overwhelming majority still were in London. However, there have been epidemics of heroin use in provincial towns.[16] A study in Crawley in 1967 showed a prevalence rate for heroin abuse of 8.5 per 1000 in the population aged 15–20, and this rose to 14.75 per 1000 when males only were considered.[17] Patterns of "initiation" have been described, with an initial contact in another town followed by a group-spread within the local community. In this case 22 out of 58 addicts were introduced to heroin in Crawley itself. Informal observations in the north-west also show clear evidence of infection through contacts in London.

Heroin abuse carries a high mortality rate. Study of 69 addict deaths up to the end of 1966 showed that before 1965 the mean age of death was 30.3, but in 1965–6 it was 24.8. 50 per cent of all deaths occurred before the age of 28. 23.2 per cent died from suicide or suicidal overdose, 29 per cent from accidental overdose or "sudden death" and 47.8 per cent from "violent deaths", septic conditions, and other "natural" causes.[18] 39 of the deaths occurred between 1955 and 1965, 35 of them male addicts and 4 female. Thus in this period 10.9 per cent of male addicts died; a death rate about 27 per 1000 per year, and twenty times the mortality rate for this age group. Of this group 5 died from suicide, 4 from suicidal overdose of other drugs than heroin, 12 from overdose of their habitual drugs, and 14 from other causes.[19] On the basis of these figures, it appears that the British heroin addicts have a mortality rate some 28 times the normal and over twice that of heroin addicts in New York: 27 per 1000 per year compared with 10 per 1000).[20]

The comparison with New York is important. The British heroin scene has been misunderstood by unintelligent application to it of American experience. There are crucial differences as well as similarities at certain points. First, the use of heroin in the United States is entirely illicit. The heroin addict is thus a criminal *per se*. Out-patient clinics were tried for a short time between 1919 and 1923 and abandoned as a failure, although some were reasonably successful. Traffic in heroin in New York is highly organized and controlled by three or four major importers.[22] In this

criminally controlled scene the whole environment in which
heroin abuse occurs is quite different from that in Britain.
Yet one still finds statements about the British scene
which seem to be based on a study of American data.[23]
Secondly, because the heroin in the United States is illicit,
it is also weak. It is unlikely that most "street addicts" in
New York are physically addicted in the sense that we know
physical addiction in Britain. Analysis of sacks of American
heroin have shown them to contain between 1–30 per cent
heroin mixed with other substances.[24] Probably most American heroin addicts use less than one grain a day. Thirdly,
the class and ethnic structure of the American scene provides a striking contrast to Britain. There are two broad
traditions of addiction within the United States, The
"Southern" white tradition of Alabama, Georgia, and
Kentucky where the average age is around the mid-forties;
and the "Northern", predominantly Negro or Puerto Rican
tradition in New York, Puerto Rico, Columbia, and
Chicago. In 1964 53·3 per cent of 55,899 addicts known to
the Federal Bureau of Narcotics were coloured. The rate
of addiction was 134 per 100,000 for negroes and 15 per
100,000 for whites. Only 4 per cent of addicts were under
21.[25] Addiction is growing faster in the Puerto Rican group
than in any other group, and between 1963–4 the percentage of Puerto Rican addicts rose from 19 per cent to
24·2 per cent of the New York total.[26] In Britain however,
under 3 per cent of addicts are coloured, and over one-
third are under 21. Fourthly, in New York addiction is
geographically concentrated in certain districts, 75 per cent
of the addicts live in 15 per cent of New York, and are
"concentrated in urban areas where poverty and despair
predominate".[27] In Britain, there are no "addict neighbourhoods" on the Harlem pattern, nor is addiction closely
related to slum districts, urban delinquent groups, or a
socially deprived minority. Finally, the American figures
show a decline from the 1920s to 100,000 addicts in the
1930s and to under 56,000 in the 1960s. The British pattern,

as shown above, has been one of slow decline followed by spectacular increases.

The British drug scene is therefore in a number of crucial respects quite unlike that in the United States. There is, however, some evidence of a movement in the American direction. For example, the traffic in drugs is tending to become more organized. There are indications of heroin abuse spreading within lower working class "twilight" areas. But, in spite of this, comparisons with New York need to be made with great caution.

2. THE NATURE OF HEROIN ADDICTION

> Junk is not, like alcohol or weed, a means to increased enjoyment of life. Junk is not a kick. It is a way of life.
> WILLIAM BURROUGHS[28]

The addict injects heroin either subcutaneously ("skin-popping") or, more commonly, intravenously, directly into the blood-stream. In the body it is broken down into morphine and by-products, and morphine is accumulated quickly in the lungs, liver, and kidneys. The nature of morphine's action is not clear, but it seems to act at the synapses in the central nervous system. After injection, the addict feels a sense of peace and drowsy euphoria. One ex-addict recorded her early feelings on heroin:

> Ever flipped out? Gone out beyond the wind? On a crystal yet brutal breeze? So that one blast could break and shatter you, yet give you such joy that you could retreat again and be happy? Once I was happy, high, high on H. A mainline fix would send me way out. But never psychic. I never cared. On hash I got high everything swam in dark, dark, dizzy waves of sheer heaven. And such bliss. And yet there was something else. Then H. Oh, my God, such heaven. Yet at first I was only elated. Pleasure. Then one day more than one jack and I got high, so high. Oh, wonderful. I hope I never forget, and that I can remember that heaven. Because it is my life. And possibly my death. But I don't care. If I could die this way I'd be happy.

Physical dependence quickly follows heroin use, although it needs to be emphasized that opiates are not universally attractive, and the fear that a large percentage of the population would conceivably be in danger of becoming addicted is false. But the euphoria described above is not long-lasting, and, as the addict becomes more dependent, so he needs to increase the dosage in order to experience the former effect. Finally, he uses the drug almost entirely to avoid the terrors of withdrawal.

The presence of an "abstinence syndrome" or "withdrawal symptoms" is the primary characteristic of physical dependence. With heroin the signs of abstinence may include yawning, rhinorrhoea, tears, sweating, anorexia (mild symptoms), trembling, goose flesh, abdominal cramps, insomnia (moderate symptoms), restlessness, vomiting, diarrhoea, and weight loss (severe symptoms).[29] Today, the worst features of the abstinence syndrome can be alleviated by use of methadone (Physeptone) and this applies in most prisons as well as in hospitals. Nevertheless, the "terrors" of withdrawal are built into the junk scene and fear of "cold turkey" goes very deep. One girl who had "come off" wrote:

It is almost impossible for someone who isn't and who never has been an addict to know what drugs mean to a junkie. A cure might sound very simple to you—the end of his troubles. But to him it's terrifying—anything he was trying to escape will come back in force. It's like being abandoned on a desert island or being in a crowded room of people whom you don't know—you feel very lost and inadequate. The actual withdrawal also scares him. You can tell him till you're blue in the face that he won't feel anything—or not too much. He won't believe you. (I don't believe people who say it doesn't hurt. The only thing I believe doesn't is narcosis. Do you remember I was frightened of going to X Hospital because they would take me off in 48 hours?) This fear can also be an excuse to stay on. If an addict really wants to come off badly enough he'll go cold turkey. But fear of withdrawal is very real—especially cold turkey, which is why the junkie is often afraid of the police, even if he hasn't done anything. Don't minimize this fear as if you were an irate parent telling your child that there were no snakes in the bed, because he'll just say "You don't understand", and he'll be right.

Lindesmith[30] has argued that addiction occurs when withdrawal distress comes to be interpreted in relation to the absence of heroin. On this view it is the overwhelming need to avoid the abstinence syndrome which is the determining factor. Wikler, who has argued that the dominant function of the opiates is to gratify "primary" needs of hunger, fear of pain, sexual urges, and so on,[31] has in his later writing moved closer to Lindesmith's stress on the central role of the abstinence syndrome. Wikler claims that, in addition to any personality disorders which may have led him to heroin abuse, the addict has acquired a set of conditioned responses, and it is this conditioning which above all contributes to the tendency to relapse. Physical symptoms associated with withdraw distress may well trigger off the appropriate response, the return to heroin.[32] It is important, therefore, not to underestimate the importance of withdrawal symptoms to the addict.

The problem of whether the origins of addiction lie in a certain type of psychological disturbance has produced varied theories, no doubt based on varied experience. The conventional cliché that the addict is seeking "escape" is a serious over-simplification. For, as Lindesmith has shown, the whole point of addiction is that heroin makes the addict feel *normal*. Does he escape his problems and inadequacies? It is a pleasantly simple theory, but not without difficulty. For "there is no evidence that such a mental state is produced in morphine addicts. There is a great deal of evidence to indicate that it is not."[33] It is alcohol and barbiturates, not opiates, which produce forgetfulness and oblivion. The heroin addict is only too well aware of the disastrous effects of his condition. Indeed, it can be claimed that the heroin addict has created more problems for himself than any he may have left behind. Nor is the argument that the addict is motivated by a search for "kicks" or for euphoria very plausible, since it is the non-addict or the "fringe" addict who derives such pleasure from the drug.

Two widely held views are, first, that it is the psychopathic personality who is most likely to become an addict, and, secondly, that the addictive condition often comes from an "attempt to avoid sexual confusion".[34] The association of addiction with psychopathy was popularized by the American writer Lawrence Kolb.[35] In Britain Glatt[36] has suggested that many addicts are psychopathic personalities, and Kirkpatrick[37] has described the addict as "a person suffering from a personality disorder of a schizoid-psychopathic type". Willis[38] agrees that "the majority of established addicts have major personality disorders", but points out that the relationship between personality disorder and addiction is not a simple one. Psychopathic personalities are probably more likely to abuse alcohol and amphetamines. If one personality type stands out among heroin addicts, it is the immature, inadequate person.[39] Unable to establish or maintain stable relationships with people, he turns to heroin for security and warmth.

The description of the heroin experience in sexual terms has been conspicuous throughout the literature of addiction.

> Over and over again one hears addicts describe the effects of the injection in sexual terms. One addict said that after a fix he felt as if he were coming from every pore. Another said that he used to inject the solution in a rhythmic fashion until it was all used up, and said that this was akin to masturbation, albeit much better.[40]

Chein and his colleagues noted the degree of sexual disturbance in their New York addicts and stressed four tendencies among them: the concern with sexual inadequacy, the deprecation of or lack of interest in sexual activity, homosexuality, and the preference of masturbation to sexual intercourse.[41] The classical psychoanalytic view of addiction is that it represents the creation of an artificial sexual model based on infantile masturbation. The process of injection replaces intercourse as the focal point of sexual experience. There is some support for this "blood orgasm" thesis in the withdrawal of many opiate addicts from ordinary sexual relationships.

In a study of a group of British female heroin addicts, D'Orban observed that "disturbed psychosexual development was one of the most striking findings".[42] Out of 66 addicts, 23 (35 per cent) were currently exclusively homosexual, 12 were transvestites, and 9 were bisexual. Homosexual orientation therefore characterized some 48 per cent of the group. Of those aged over 21, the percentage was 58 per cent, of those under 21 only 21 per cent. The homosexual orientation had generally predated drug abuse and was not seen as causally related to their involvement in the drug scene. D'Orban significantly commented:[43]

> Viewed in the context of their personality change as shown by their disturbed delinquent and grossly unstable conduct, their often profound lack of self-esteem and their obvious emotional deprivation, their heroin dependence appeared almost a minor symptom and could be regarded as but the most recent development in their long history of maladjustment.[43]

Certainly there are few heroin addicts who do not show severe emotional and psychological problems. To view them simply as "addicts" is to isolate their drug use in so artificial a manner as to make it the central feature of their disturbed condition, rather than as the most painful symptom of their underlying need.

In Britain, there seems little indication that heroin addiction is related significantly to violent crime, although there is no doubt that some violent people may become heroin addicts.[44] However, there is considerable evidence that many addicts have records of criminal behaviour prior to their involvement with drugs. Of the sample of 50 male addict prisoners studied by I. P. James,[45] 22 had juvenile court convictions, 16 more had adult court convictions, while 7 had been convicted before the age of thirteen. Altogether three-quarters showed a history of court convictions prior to addiction. Similarly, D'Orban's study of female addict prisoners[46] showed that 40 of the 66 (60 per cent) had court appearances prior to addiction, while 32 per cent had been in approved schools and 30 per cent in borstal. Altogether 57 (86 per cent) of the group had previous convictions. But the most common offences were larceny, receiving, and housebreaking, and there was a good deal of delinquency. Where there was aggression and violence, it was due to use of methylamphetamine, not heroin.

The "treatment" of addiction, therefore, is inseparable from the treatment of the deep-rooted personality disorders which the addict manifests. The management of the physical withdrawal syndrome is in itself a relatively straightforward matter, the normal method being to reduce the amount of heroin and to substitute methadone (Physeptone), perhaps first by injection, and then in tablet or linctus form. On an out-patient basis, the use of large amounts of oral methadone acts as a heroin antagonist or blockade, and this has become known as a "methadone maintenance" programme, based on the work of Dole and Nyswander in the United States.[46] Cyclazocine has also been used in the United States. This drug (2-cyclopropylmethyl-2-hydroxy-5,9-dimethyl-6,7-bensomorphan) is a narcotic antagonist in the benzomorphan series. If given to addicts it precipitates severe abstinence symptoms, apparently by occupying the opiate receptor sites in the central nervous system and so preventing them from acting.[47] Other "physical" methods used in Britain in selected cases have included stereotactic surgery[48] and aversion therapy[49]

But the most important and most difficult aspect of "treatment" is the care of the addict within the community. In the United States, the Ramirez programme involves the use of trained ex-addicts, and a rehabilitation process extending over some two years.[50] Synanon, Daytop, and Phoenix Houses use ex-addicts in a highly structured and authoritarian setting.[51] In Britain, there has been little progress so far in tackling the social and environmental aspects of addiction, although the Report of the Sub-Committee on Rehabilitation[52] sees "the out-patient clinics as being strategically placed to form the focal point for the whole process of rehabitation". Any approach which sees opiate addiction in purely clinical terms is certain to achieve little.

4
The "Pot" Scene

More has been written about cannabis than
is known about it.   DR M. M. GLATT[1]

Cannabis sativa is the name of the hemp plant which grows
throughout the world. From the tops of the female plant
as it is about to flower is derived a green resinous substance
which ceases when the seeds have ripened. In tropical
climates the resin is plentiful. From the flowering tops of
the plant comes the drug known as bhang in India, ganga
in the West Indies, dagga in South Africa, kif in Morocco,
takrouri in Tunisia, and marijuana in the United States
and Britain. The resin is known as hashish in Arab coun-
tries, the United States and Britain, esrar in Turkey, and
charas in India. There are numerous other names. In
Britain, marijuana is referred to as "pot" or "grass", and
hashish (cannabis resin) as "hash", and it is hashish which
is most common here. It is the resin which contains most
of the active chemical principles and therefore is the most
potent. Marijuana or ganga, the dried flowering and fruited
tops of the plant, is stronger in effect than bhang, the dried
leaves and flower shoots of both male and female plants,
wild or cultivated.

The word "cannabis" has been traced to the Assyrians
who used the drug as incense in the seventh and eighth
centuries B.C. They called it "Qunubu" or "Qunnabu"
from the old East Iranian "Konaba" which was identical
with the Greek "Konabos", meaning "noise".[2] "Marijuana"
perhaps is derived from the Mexican-Spanish "mariguana"

or the Portuguese "mariguango", meaning "an intoxicant", or from the Mexican-Spanish slang "Mary Jane".[3] References in ancient writings are frequent. The Zend-Avesta in the sixth century B.C. mentioned its existence in Persia, and it was suggested in the last century that Ezekiel was high on cannabis when he experienced the vision of chapter 1, and that Nebuchadnezzar fed on the drug ("grass").[4] The Chinese carved hard hemp stalks into snakes' heads and used them against evil spirits. Hao-Tho, around A.D. 220 used cannabis as an anaesthetic, mixing the resin with wine, and called it Ma-lo.[5] It played an important role in Indian religion and philosophy and has been used for centuries by ascetics as an aid to concentration and prayer.[6] "The mere sight of bhang", claims a Bengali sect, "cleanses from us as much sin as a thousand horse sacrifices."

The spread of cannabis on a significant scale in Britain is a post-war phenomenon. But as early as 1938 press reports referred to Soho as a source of supply,[7] and there were further references to Soho in 1948[8] as well as to Liverpool's Chinese community as centres of cannabis smoking.[9] In 1949 it was reported that cannabis was being grown commercially in greenhouses in Liverpool,[10] and in 1950, twenty people were arrested in raids on a Soho club and dance hall.[11] Also in 1950, 26 kg. of hashish were found, only the second time that hashish had been found in Britain.[12] After the murder of Joseph Aaku, the "king of the dope pedlars", Scotland Yard in 1952 reported that they had uncovered a chain of sellers throughout Britain.[13] In the same year appeared the first British study, a curiously inaccurate work entitled *Indian Hemp: A Social Menace* by Donald McI. Johnson. In 1955, Banton[14] referred to the use of cannabis among West African café groups in the Cable Street area of Stepney. In 1956 one Stephen Ward, in a lecture to the Women's Adjustment Board, introduced a recipe for hashish fudge, and this curious recipe survives in a well-known paperback cookery book.[15]

Cannabis was first placed under international control by the Geneva Convention of 1925, and this was superseded by the Single Convention of 1961. But in Britain its use, until the mid-fifties, was largely confined to immigrant communities, merchant seamen, and others in ports and dockland areas, jazz musicians, and members of fringe proto-beatnik worlds. As late as 1966 Bewley could claim,[15a] though by this time quite wrongly, that "users of cannabis are generally either recent immigrants or belong to a 'beatnik' subculture". By 1954 there were more convictions of white persons for possession of cannabis, and by 1964 whites were in the majority (see Table 1). By this time, the bulk

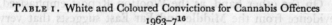

	1963	1964	1965	1966	1967
White	296	284	400	767	1737
Coloured	367	260	226	352	656

TABLE 1. White and Coloured Convictions for Cannabis Offences 1963–7[16]

of the traffic involved hashish and much of it consisted of amateur smuggling from Lebanon, Pakistan, and Cyprus. Smoking was increasing among students from 1961 onwards, and there was some selling of cannabis during the Aldermaston March of 1963.[16a] A spread down the socioeconomic scale was also evident, and more working-class adolescents were involved.

Nomenclature and classification is a confusing field. Cannabis has been described as a mild hallucinogen and included among the "psychotomimetic" drugs, that is, drugs which precipitate an imitation psychosis.[17] It is misleading to describe it as a narcotic and link it with opiates, for its nature and effects are completely different. The international literature is almost unanimous in stressing that it is not a drug of addiction, in the sense of physical dependence, nor does it produce tolerance,[18] though severe psychological dependence has been reported.[19] The Wootton Report which concluded that "the long-term consumption of cannabis in moderate doses has no harmful effects"[20] was not, as has been claimed, expressing an original viewpoint. The Indian Hemp Commission of 1893–4 reported that "there is no evidence of any weight regarding mental and moral injury from moderate use of the drugs" and that "the evidence shows the moderate use of ganja or charas not to be appreciably harmful".[21] Similarly, the Mayor of New York's Committee reported in 1944 that "those who had been smoking marihuana for a period of years showed no mental or physical deterioration which may be attributed to the drug".[22] Possibly the pharmacological action of cannabis is to increase the serotonin content of the brain but to antagonize its peripheral action, and this may produce a psychotomimetic effect.[23] But there are no lasting ill effects as a direct result even of the acute use of cannabis[24] and it is best described as "a relatively mild intoxicant".[25]

On the other hand, as the Wootton Report emphasized, evidence from the Middle and Far East suggests that very heavy long-term consumption may lead to "a syndrome of increasing mental and physical deterioration".[26] "It is not possible", the Report continued[27] "to say that long continued consumption, medically or for pleasure, of cannabis . . . is free from possible danger." The ill-effects associated with chronic abuse must be seen in relation to the interaction of the drug, the personality, and the environment. As was stressed in the previous chapter, it is misleading to isolate and exaggerate the importance of the drug *per se* when one is concerned with a highly disturbed personality or deviant group.

The immediate physical and psychological effects of cannabis have frequently been described. The effects of moderate use are in fact mainly psychological and may last from two to three hours. There may be an increased awareness of colours and sounds with an increased sensitivity, a feeling of euphoria and excitement, followed by tranquillity and peacefulness, and perhaps sleep. Some users value the drug primarily for its hypnotic effect. In some people, however, depression and anxiety may result, since cannabis intensifies the current mood of the user. Physical effects are limited to a reddening of the eyes and some irritation of the throat and perhaps the chest. The recent controlled experiments by Zinberg and his colleagues showed a moderate increase in heart rate, but no change in the respiratory rate, in pupil size, or in blood sugar levels.[28] There have, however, been a few reports of very heavy intake, including one of intravenous use,[29] with subsequent vomiting, diarrhoea, abdominal cramps, vertigo, conjugate deviation of the eyes, hypotension, respiratory failure, and collapse.

The potency of cannabis depends upon the amount of the active chemical principles contained in it. Hashish is more potent than marijuana, and it has been estimated that the marijuana smoked in the United States is between one-fifth and one-eighth the strength of Indian charas.[30] Some of the American studies which have reported mild effects have involved marijuana.

The comparison of hashish and marijuana is like that between pure alcohol and beer. Lurid accounts of the psychological effects and dangers of hemp are often based upon observations made by and upon hashish users.[31]

But in Britain it is hashish from the Lebanon which is most common. However, as smoked, marijuana and hashish are probably of comparable strength. One London doctor has claimed that the transition from "pot" to "hash" among London smokers some years ago brought about a marked change in the symptoms observed. With "pot" these were simply mild euphoria, altered time perception, and the ability to concentrate on abstract detail. The drug was used by some as an anti-depressant, and there were few hangovers. With "hash", however, there has been an increase in headaches, visual difficulties, hunger pangs (leading to a frantic consumption of cornflakes!) and anxiety about paranoid reactions.[32]

Analysis of hashish between 1930 and 1942 yielded three types of related compounds: cannabidiol, cannabinol, and tetrahydrocannabinol (THC). It is now believed that the main active component of cannabis is Δ^9-tetrahydrocannabinol (sometimes referred to as Δ^1-tetrahydrocannabinol, and from now on cited as THC).[33] In 1967, Isbell and his colleagues in the United States published "the first demonstration of hashish-like activity of a tetrahydrocannabinol of known chemical structure in man".[34] In Britain, the Soma Research Association is conducting research on THC, and this will help considerably to clarify the confusing data about the effects of cannabis and its pharmacological action in man.

There have been many claims that cannabis enhances creative, literary, artistic, and musical ability. The American beatnik poets used it in the search for enlightenment and as an aid to composition.[35] William Burroughs has claimed that it is valuable in the early stages of writing because it stimulates association patterns in the brain.[36] In New York it has been claimed that "almost all modern jazz musicians have used marijuana at one time or another"[37] and its influence on the post-1920 jazz scene is obvious. In Britain moderate use of cannabis plays a role in the pop and folk worlds. But not all observers are impressed by the claims made for it. "Cannabis users claim always to be full of ideas," observed Glatt[38] "but they hardly ever seem to come round to translating them into constructive actions." Nor are the doubts confined to those outside the "pot" scene. A hippy magazine recently complained that cannabis was making the so-called revolutionaries ineffective. The writer claimed that "its narcotic effects tend to be cumulative" and that chronic users show "a lack of interest in communicating about anything except the drug".[39] This is also a common left-wing viewpoint.

Other claims about cannabis have stressed its therapeutic possibilities. One London doctor has used it, in tincture form, in the treatment of certain emotional states and, although the British Pharmaceutical Codex regards it as "too unreliable in action to be of value in therapeutics"[40] it has been suggested that it could be of use in psychotherapy and as an antibiotic.[41] A pharmacologist writing in 1941 expressed the view that "a good preparation of hemp is incomparably the best drug for depressive mental conditions",[42] but it is doubtful whether many today would view it as of value in medicine.

Two major aspects of the cannabis controversy centre around the questions of "cannabis psychosis" and of "escalation" from cannabis to heroin, and the evidence on these questions will now be considered.

(a) Cannabis and Psychosis

> Chronic intake causes a characteristic chronic psychosis.
>
> DR ELIZABETH TYLDEN[43]

> Cannabis does not produce psychoses.
>
> DR O. MORAES ANDRADE[44]

It has been claimed that cannabis is a "psychotogenic" drug, and in 1967 Tylden[45] warned of "the beginning of a crop of cannabis psychotics".

> There are innumerable articles about the cannabis psychosis. Some of them are of considerable antiquity, but the state observed today is clearly recognizable from them. In this century there are reliable accounts of cannabis psychosis from India, America, Brazil, Morocco, U.S.S.R., and more recently the U.K.[46]

Reports from Morocco, India and Nigeria seem to confirm this.[47] Benabud speaks of "mass addiction" and "cannabis psychosis",[48] while the Chopras refer to "cannabis insanity".[49] Asuni's observations in Nigeria[50] showed schizophrenia to be common among cannabis smokers admitted as hospital patients there. When these reports are scrutinized, however, it is clear that cannabis is simply one factor in a complex social structure. In Benabud's Morocco study there is a close link between the "psychosis" and social conditions, for 57 per cent of the "kif addicts" admitted as patients in 1956 came from Casablanca, the district with the poorest conditions and highest rate of overcrowding.[51] Similarly, the Chopras admit that it was hard to ascertain if cannabis was "only secondary to the existing mental disorder" and they stress that moderate use does not lead to insanity unless some predisposing factor is present.[52] As was seen earlier the Indian Hemp Drugs Commission of 1893–1894 found no evidence of mental and moral injury from moderate consumption of cannabis.[53] A report from South Africa admitted that dagga produced "occasional psychotic episodes" but stressed that alcohol was guilty of "even graver action".[54] Andrade, of the Ministry of Health in Brazil, denies the existence of a specific cannabis psychosis.[44]

In the American literature, psychoses have have been rarely described. Becker noted:[55]

> Marihuana first began to be used in the United States in the 1920s and early 30s, and all reports of psychosis associated with its use date from approximately that period. A search of both *Psychological Abstracts* and the *Cumulative Index Medicus* (and its predecessors, the *Current List of Medical Literature* and the *Quarterly Index Medicus*) revealed no cases after 1940.

Becker sees "psychotic episodes" as occurring less frequently within a culture as the drug spreads and the range of possible effects becomes understood. The incidence of psychosis, on this view, is a function of the stage of development of drug-using cultures.[56] In general American studies hold the view expressed in 1942 by Allentuck and Bowman[57] that "a characteristic marihuana psychosis does not exist. Marihuana will not produce a psychosis *de novo* in a well-integrated stable person", and this is the view taken by the Wootton Committee in Britain.[58]

Sir Aubrey Lewis, in a valuable review of the clinical literature, observed:[59]

Cannabis psychoses have been frequently described and the accounts include practically every known variety of mental disorder. . . . The term "cannabis psychosis" begs the question of the existence of such a syndrome.

In fact "verified reports of drug-induced psychosis are scarcer than one might think"[60] and in many cases the "psychosis" is a panic reaction to the drug experience. Particularly when heavy doses are involved the drug may precipitate a psychotic reaction, so that "the line between marihuana intoxication and an incipient psychosis is difficult to define".[61] However, there is some support for Tylden's view in the report of Isbell's THC experiments. Isbell concluded:[62]

It has long been known that marihuana and hashish can cause psychotic reactions, but usually such reactions were ascribed to individual idiosyncrasies rather than being usual or common reactions to the drug. The data in these experiments, however, definitely indicate that the psychotomimetic effects of Δ^1-THC are dependent on dosage and that sufficiently high doses can cause psychotic reactions in almost any individual.

The fact that such psychotic reactions are rare in the United States "may reflect nothing more than the low tetrahydrocannabinol content of most of the marihuana available in the United States".[63] If this were so we should expect a higher incidence of psychotic episodes in the British "hash" scene. There seems little indication of this so far.

Two conclusions seem to follow from this evidence. First, that heavy dosages of cannabis *can* help to bring about a psychotic condition. Secondly, that the term "cannabis psychosis" is not a particularly helpful one since probably the role of the drug is to trigger off a mental reaction which may be one of a variety of types. Thirdly, that the consideration of dosage, personality and environment are crucial to any understanding of this "psychotomimetic" action.

(b) Cannabis and Escalation

Close parallelism between curves can be notoriously uninformative.   DR C. R. B. JOYCE[64]

The argument for an "escalation" from cannabis to the
opiates has two versions. The first, the crude (and demon-
strably false) version, is that use of cannabis gradually, in
most cases, leads the user to take heroin. The second, the
more common and more intelligent version, is that, through
association with an illicit drug scene, the cannabis user will
be brought into contact with opiate addiction. In this
form, the argument can be used either for or against the
present situation, for one could, on this premise, argue
either than cannabis must be treated more harshly by sanct-
ions, or that to legalize cannabis would be to cut the link
with opiate addiction. The first version can be quickly
dismissed. The vast majority of cannabis users, both
throughout the world and in Britain do not go on to
heroin.[65] (If they did, the British heroin figures would show
an increase far beyond the present number, and a large
percentage of the addicts would be coloured.) But what of
the second version? Three specific points need to be made,
one logical, the others factual.

First, there is a difference between saying that the increases in cannabis use and in heroin addiction are connected, and saying that they are *causally* connected. Many
writers have pointed to the parallelism between cannabis
convictions and heroin notifications between 1959 and 1967
(though not during 1962–5). This association in itself proves
nothing. Before the war the curves for first admission rates
to mental hospitals, *per capita* consumption of bananas,
and the number of wireless licences issued by the G.P.O.
paralleled each other closely. Again, to say that a young
person *started* on cannabis and later became addicted to
heroin is not to say that he "escalated" from one to the
other. The word "escalation" is a loaded word and its use
can easily lead one to read the conclusion of the argument

into the premise. Most methylated spirit drinkers *started*
on beer or cheap wines.

Secondly, the argument that cannabis users are *auto-
matically* brought into contact with heroin addicts is simply
not true. This depends on the area and the circumstances.
Certainly it is true to say, in general terms, that

> Abuse of cannabis facilitates the association with social groups
> and subcultures involved with more dangerous drugs such as
> opiates or barbiturates. Transition to the use of such drugs
> would be a consequence of this association rather than an
> inherent effect of cannabis.[66]

But in many districts, the cannabis user has no association
with heroin addicts. Goode in the United States has pointed
out that the association of cannabis with heroin, the "narcotics cycle", only applies in the New York slum drug
pattern, whereas in many other areas the association is
between cannabis and other hallucinogenic agents. Of 200
cannabis users interviewed by Goode, only 27 (13 per cent)
had taken heroin, whereas 99 (49 per cent) had taken LSD
and 87 (43 per cent) had taken amphetamines. In London,
there is a good deal of evidence that the psychedelically-
orientated cannabis users have been moving further and
further away from the hard drug scene, and, if anything, a
kind of "de-escalation" process has been in operation. The
Wootton Report observed that "supplies of cannabis are
not necessarily obtained in the same places as heroin".[68]

Thirdly, the fact that all, or more, heroin addicts have
used cannabis is probably less significant than it seems. It is
no answer to the "escalation" thesis to say that all heroin
addicts have also drunk coffee or smoked tobacco or gone to
state schools: for the point of the argument is that cannabis
smoking, unlike these other activities, is restricted to a
small, though increasing, percentage of the population, and
it is from within this minority that all the new heroin
addicts have come. But to say this is to say no more than
that they have come from within that broad spectrum of
adolescent society within which cannabis, *along with many*

other things, is accepted. The crucial question is whether there is any factor inherent either in the pharmacology of cannabis or in the subcultural groups associated with its use which would tend to lead the user towards heroin. The answer to both questions seems to be negative. Cannabis and heroin are pharmacologically unrelated. Moreover, to talk of a single "cannabis subculture" is grossly misleading, since the most striking feature of the use of cannabis has been its spread throughout all classes and sections of society. But even within the adolescent "pot" scenes there are many pressures, psychological, social, cultural, which would tend to go against the likelihood of heroin abuse. The forces which lead most users to smoke cannabis are quite unlike those which lead to heroin. Studies both among provincial heroin users[69] and among young drifters in London[70] have failed to justify the escalation thesis. Indeed, there is some evidence that if any pattern of progression is significant it is that from the amphetamines to opiates. In D'Orban's prison sample of heroin addicts 64 per cent had used cannabis and 65 per cent amphetamines.[71] In Soho, the crucial link between the fringe drug taker and the junkie subculture was not cannabis but methylamphetamine. This has not been a simple "escalation", but rather an alternating process, with heroin replacing amphetamines but later being replaced by amphetamines again, and so on.

The truth behind the escalation thesis is that cannabis users are more likely to become heroin addicts than non-cannabis users. In view of the apparent and increasing spread of cannabis and of the social and cultural traditions associated with its use, this is likely to become less and less significant an axiom as the years go on. Heroin addiction is more likely to be averted by attention to the underlying personal problems of the potential addict than by concern about cannabis or any other external features present within the scene. The abuse of cannabis raises its own problems which are quite different from those raised by heroin addiction.

5

The Acid Scene

Whenever in doubt, turn off your mind, relax, float downstream.

LEARY, METZNER, AND ALPERT,
The Psychedelic Experience[1]

Turn off your mind, relax, and float downstream.
This is not dying.   THE BEATLES, "Revolver"

It was a British physician Humphrey Osmond who first
defined the word "psychedelic".

A psychedelic compound is one like LSD or mescaline which
enriches the mind and enlarges the vision. It is this kind of
experience which provides the greatest possibility for examin-
ing those areas most interesting to psychiatry and which has
provided men down the ages with experiences they have considered valuable above all others.[2]

The existence of "psychedelic" drugs has been known
for centuries. The peyote cactus (lophophora Williamsii)
was used in native Mexican religions as a sacred element,
and during the nineteenth century Indian tribes reintro-
duced the peyote to the United States from raids in
northern Mexico. The visual hallucinations derived from
peyote are due to the presence of mescaline, and it was
mescaline which provided the basis for the two dominant
approaches to these drugs. First, the approach which sees
them as "psychedelic", enriching the mind and enlarging
the vision, and perhaps capable of use in mystical and
religious experience. Aldous Huxley has been seen as the

Western prophet of "the chemical conditions of transcendental experience",[3] but it should be noted that Havelock Ellis discussed the "new artificial paradise" of mescaline in 1897.[4] The implications of this view will be discussed more fully in chapter 8.

The second approach sees these drugs as valuable models for the understanding of schizophrenia. Because they were held to bring about a "model psychosis" they became known as "psychotomimetics". A study in 1940 argued that mescaline brought about a psychosis, and suggested that non-organic psychoses were in fact variants of the same disease, perhaps caused by an amine resembling mescaline. If this were the case, then the correct approach to understanding the nature and treatment of the psychotic diseases lay in the fields of biochemistry and pharmacology.[5]

The discovery of lysergic acid diethylamine (LSD) by Hofmann in 1938 was the crucial event in the "psychedelic revolution". Lysergic acid is derived from ergot, and LSD is its diethylamide derivative. Later in 1943 Hofmann, through accidentally ingesting and inhaling LSD, found it to have hallucinogenic properties. He wrote that "fantastic visions of extraordinary vividness accompanied by a kaleidoscopic play of intense coloration continuously swirled around me".[6] Since then LSD has been used clinically and more recently has entered illicit use in what has become known in the United States and Britain as the "acid scene". In this illicit context the drug circulates either as a liquid soaked on a sugar cube, on blotting paper, or, more commonly now, in blue pills.

The therapeutic use of LSD was introduced in Britain at Powick Hospital by Dr R. A. Sandison, a psychiatrist with a Jungian background, around 1954. Sandison saw that through the use of LSD, the patient could relive his experiences during the first year of life. The use of LSD in this way has been described in Britain at length by Lake who stressed its advantages over methylamphetamine and other agents, in that the situations brought to consciousness by other drugs have usually occurred much later than the first year of life.

> The advantage of LSD is that by its use the patient is often enabled to proceed *direct* to the painful first year experience so as to discharge its buried emotions of anxiety and anger *in its original context*. It is in the hours of psychosynthesis which follow the abreaction that the later incidents which had touched off the primal anxiety are often readily brought to mind. Now that the primal emotion has been remembered, their own repression is no longer necessary. It is for this reason that we now favour LSD rather than the other abreactive agents.[7]

Various writers have claimed that LSD has been particularly valuable in the treatment of sexual disorders, anxiety states, psychoneuroses, and psychopathic conditions.[8]

The uncontrolled illicit use of LSD presents very complex problems. In New York, Louria has reported severe psychiatric disturbances induced by LSD and needing prolonged hospitalization. The major manifestations were confusion, visual and auditory hallucinations, and, in about one-seventh, overwhelming terrifying panic. Louria claims that "there can then be no doubt that LSD can produce psychosis in a previously 'normal, well-adjusted' individual".[9] A Canadian study of 225 adverse reactions to LSD prior to June 1967 showed that 142 were cases of prolonged psychotic conditions with paranoid delusions, schizophrenic-like hallucinations, and overwhelming fear.[10] Sidney Cohen, perhaps the leading American authority, has classified possible LSD complications under three heads. First, psychotic disorders, including the accidental intoxication of children, chronic intoxications, schizophrenic reactions, paranoia, acute paranoid states, prolonged or intermittent LSD-like psychosis, and psychotic depressions. Secondly, non-psychotic disorders, including chronic anxiety reactions with depression, somatic symptoms and difficulties in functioning, acute panic states, dyssocial and anti-social behaviour.

Thirdly, neurological reactions, including convulsions and permanent brain damage.[11]

What exactly is the LSD experience? Three elements in it seem to be dominant. First, the effect of a kaleidoscope of intense light and colour, bringing with it the intensifying of experience through all the senses. Leary's instructions to the psychedelic initiate include this passage:[12]

> You are now witnessing the magical dance of forms.
> Ecstatic kaleidoscopic patterns explode all round you.
> All possible shapes come to life before your eyes,
> The retinal circus.
> The ceaseless play of elements—
> Earth, water, air, fire—
> In ever-changing forms and manifestations,
> Dazzles you with its complexity and variety.

The use of the word "hallucinogenic" can be misleading about this experience, since true hallucinations are not necessarily produced by LSD, auditory ones occurring even less frequently than visual. (This suggests "an important difference between LSD-induced psychoses and the naturally occurring ones, such as schizophrenia where patients are more prone to hear voices than to see little men on the wall".[13] Rather the pattern is one of perceptual change, the distortion and expansion of sense experiences, and "synesthesia"—the translation of one sense into another.

Secondly, there is the element of depersonalization, of ego-loss. Sandison described this experience as "a sort of detached ego".[14] The conscious self is separated from the body and there is a symbolic disintegration of the real world. It is at this point that the psychotic and the mystical experience come very close, for in both there is the transcendence of the ego. In fact, it has been suggested that in the LSD experience the individual undergoes an experimental psychosis by which he may be positively enriched.[15] In the transcendence of the ego is the fundamental characteristic of the psychedelic experience.

Thirdly, there is the illumination of reality and of the universe. This one might describe as the spiritual dimension of psychedelics. Leary and his colleagues in *The Psychedelic Experience* make this claim:[15]

> A psychedelic experience is a journey to new realms of consciousness. The scope and content of the experience is limitless, but its characteristic features are the transcendence of verbal concepts, of space-time dimensions, and of the ego or identity. Such experiences of enlarged consciousness can occur in a variety of ways: sensory deprivation, yoga exercises, disciplined meditation, religious or aesthetic ecstasies, or spontaneously. Most recently they have become available to anyone through the ingestion of psychedelic drugs such as LSD, psilocybin, mescaline, DMT, etc.

Of course, not all those who experiment with LSD are conscious of profound spiritual need or a desire for "meta-egoic" experiences. Indeed it is precisely their lack of preparedness for the experience which produces so many casualties. Allan Y. Cohen, from experience in California, comments that he has seen "cases of those who have gotten lost in inner space and 'flipped out', perhaps never to return a whole person".[17] Many of the psychoses seem to occur when the unprepared person is faced with the terrors of ego-loss combined with an inability to return to ordinary consciousness. This brings a terrifying panic and fear.

Recently there were reports of genetic damage from LSD and this, combined with a number of "bad trips" reduced the popularity of illicit use towards the end of 1967.[19] The beginning of 1969, however, saw a revival of LSD consumption within London, but on a small scale and so far without many very severe casualties. Nevertheless the dangers of irresponsible use of this substance are still very apparent.

Three other potent hallucinogenic drugs, popular in the United States and to a lesser extent in Britain, are psilocybin, bufotenine, and dimethyltryptamine, each of these being closely related chemically to serotonin. Other allegedly more powerful agents have appeared from time to time, such as STP and TMA. STP was hailed as a hallucinogen more potent and more dangerous than LSD and warnings were given by some observers that STP "bad trips" must not under any circumstances be treated with chlorpromazine (Largactil) or the phenothiazines, the standard method with LSD. STP was identified with DOM (2,5-dimethoxy-4-methyl-amphetamine), a substance chemically related to mescaline but about one hundred times more potent. However, an American study pointed out that the minimum hallucinogenic dose of mescaline was 300 mg. and of LSD 0·1 mg. and concluded therefore that "DOM is only above one-thirtieth as potent as LSD".[20] Moreover, black-market STP probably contained only about 10 mg. of DOM per pill. Two studies reported that "there was no accentuation of any DOM effects by chlorpromazine".[21] TMA, similar in structure, was studied in America in 1964.[22] Most of these agents have only a limited circulation in the British drug scene. Also it is probable that not all the substances have been correctly identified: for instance, the reports of adverse effects of phenothiazines after "STP" psychosis are too frequent to be without basis, and it seems likely that one is dealing with a number of different chemicals under the same black market description.

The irresponsible use of "psychedelic" drugs is not a new phenomenon. It has been suggested that the origin of the term "going berserk" (berserkgang) in ancient Scandinavian history was associated with the abuse by warriors of a hallucinogenic mushroom containing bufotenine.[23] "Going berserk" is a fair description of the adverse reactions to LSD by many young people. Some simple advice about help over such crises is given in chapter 7. It needs to be emphasized that the use of LSD requires a properly controlled environment, what Leary calls "set" and "setting", in which the user is guided through his experience, and that the conditions of safety in a therapeutic setting certainly do not apply in most of the illicit use. Although in most cases the LSD psychosis disappears in about two days, there are many instances where hallucinations may recur with intensity days, weeks, or even months after the LSD was taken, in spite of the fact that no further drugs had been used. The biochemical reason for this recurrence is not known. Moreover, evidence shows clearly that LSD is being used by young people with severe psychiatric disturbances, and these are precisely the group with whom the drug can be disastrously harmful. Cases of deaths from jumping out of windows or from roof-tops after taking LSD are not unknown.[24] Finally, it needs to be said that, however "illuminated" or "expanded" they may be, the "acid-heads" invariably become obsessed with the search for newer and better drug experiences, and cease to be useful members, not only of the society out of which they have contracted (which is understandable), but also of the society to which they belong. They are looked upon, both by the "scene" and by the "straights" (conventional people) as tragic, disintegrated, damaged persons.

PART TWO

Pastoral Care
in the Drug Scene

... the Lord has anointed me to bring good tidings to the afflicted; he has sent me to bind up the brokenhearted, to proclaim liberty to the captives, and the opening of the prison to those who are bound.   *Isaiah 61.1* (R.S.V.)

6

The Social Structure of the Drug Scene

1. THE SOCIOLOGY OF CANNABIS USE

Everybody must get stoned. BOB DYLAN

It was Lenny Bruce who commented that cannabis would soon be legalized because the law students were now smoking it.[1] In both the United States and Britain in recent years the most striking feature of cannabis use has been its spread geographically into sections of society which had previously no involvement in the drug scene. It is no longer possible to speak of a "typical" cannabis user. But this spread is, in Britain, a very recent phenomenon, and several years ago it was quite possible to delineate a number of quite clear patterns among cannabis users, who altogether comprised a very small proportion of the population.

Three traditions in particular have been historically associated with cannabis use. The first was the beatnik tradition with its sources of inspiration in such poets as Ginsberg and Ferlinghetti and such writers as Lawrence Lipton[2] and Jack Kerouac.[3] The beatniks of the purist tradition, as opposed to what Lipton dismissed as the "hip squares", phoney beats, hoodlums, junkies and so on,[4] were concerned about freedom, enlightenment, pleasure, and spirituality. Their use of cannabis was an integral part of their life-style.

The euphoria that the beats who use marijuana are seeking

is not the wholly passive, sedative pacifying experience that
the users of the commercial tranquillisers want. On the contrary they are looking for a greater source of aliveness, a
heightened sense of awareness.[5]

Lipton describes the "pot" experience as a "metaphysical
orgasm"[6] and relates its use to the role played by Zen in the
beat philosophy. In Britain by the 1950s cannabis was in
use among the more *avant garde* of beat poets and writers,
at least in London.

The second tradition of cannabis use was the jazz tradition, and from within the jazz world many of the slang
terms originated which later became part of the "pot"
scene. An American writer has pointed out that "almost all
modern jazz musicians have used marijuana at one time
or another",[7] claiming that around 23 per cent of New
York jazz musicians were regular users and 54 per cent
occasional smokers. There was also a tradition of heroin
addiction among jazz musicians, "amounting perhaps to
some 16 per cent in New York by the end of the 1950s".[8] In
the New Orleans period of jazz in the early twentieth century, alcohol was the main intoxicant used. Cannabis came
into prominence in the 1920s in Kansas City, Chicago and
New York, and titles such as "Hophead", "Muggles",
"Reefer Song", "Viper's Drag", "Sweet Marijuana Brown",
and "Weed Smokers Dream" witness to its influence. In
Britain, cannabis was probably originally smoked in jazz
clubs, and again there is a small minority of jazz musicians
among heroin addicts.

The third tradition has been immigrants from West and
North Africa, India, Pakistan, and the Caribbean. The
earliest geographical "clusterings" ("concentrations" is too
strong a term) of cannabis users were around ports and
dockland areas, and particularly in café quarters. Such
areas as Moss Side in Manchester, Liverpool 8, Bute Town
in Cardiff, and Cable Street in Stepney were examples of
districts where in the late 1940s cannabis smoking was common among small groups of immigrants and seamen. Ban-

ton in his study of Cable Street in 1955[9] referred to the use of cannabis there, and it is certain that by the late 1950s there was a well-organized traffic which fed the Cable Street market. But those involved in this café subculture were mainly immigrants from Gambia, Sierra Leone, Nigeria, and Somalia, with an increasing involvement of Indians, Pakistanis, and West Indians as the years went on. There were few instances of English adolescents involved until 1964 and 1965. It is interesting that some of the original dealers from this period in the East End of London have now moved "up West", a more profitable and expanding market.

The cannabis scene until the early 1960s did not noticeably affect the working-class adolescent, delinquent or non-delinquent. In a study of delinquent subcultures in the Stepney area published in 1966 (but on the basis of research in 1960), Downes commented that the "retreatist" pattern of drug use was "hip", upper class, middle class, or "student" class rather than connected with working-class subcultural delinquency. But, he added, "this is not to deny the probability of the drug-cult spreading down the socio-economic scale".[10] It is noticeable that Downes's study included the Cable Street area with its long tradition of cannabis use within a restricted circle.

By 1965 the word "subculture" was being used, sometimes rather loosely, about the drug scene. Earlier writers had denied the existence of a "drug subculture" in Britain and had seen its absence as one of the marked characteristics of the British, as opposed to the American, pattern. Thus Schur in 1963 wrote:[11]

> As one might expect, there has been no pronounced development in Great Britain of an "addict subculture". . . . In Great Britain the condition of addiction does not, in other words, necessarily imply membership in an addict subculture.

Schur was writing here specifically of narcotic addicts, but his comment was typical of many about the drug scene as a whole. Downes[12] criticized the application of American subcultural theory to Britain, and pointed out that much of the American writing on delinquency was inseparable from its concept of the role of the "gang". By 1965 and 1966, however, there were clear signs of drug subcultures emerging. As will be shown below, there were several quite distinct subcultural groups associated with drug use which appeared. The cannabis scene specifically was affected by three sets of events.

First, immigration from the "coloured Commonwealth" increased markedly in 1961 and 1962. A certain percentage of these newcomers came from areas where the use of cannabis was an accepted part of their lives, and until 1964 the majority of those convicted of cannabis offences were coloured immigrants. Secondly, in the early 1960s the violent, aggressive mood of the "rock and roll" epoch which had been initiated by Bill Haley and the Comets in 1954 gave way to a more tranquil, pacifist mood. Many young people marched from Aldermaston, and the Campaign of Nuclear Disarmament became the focal point for the most powerful forces of adolescent protest and idealism. This non-violent movement brought about a new youth culture based on the rejection of war and violence, and the concern for new values. Resistance to convention, bureaucracy, and the "Establishment", and the assertion of individual conscience and freedom were fundamental elements. It was a tradition within which cannabis smoking could easily find a place. The slogan "Burn Pot, Not People" was a natural, though not inevitable, corollary of "Make Love, Not War". Thirdly, the growth of contemporary folk music articulated much of the protest and the striving of this new youth culture. The songs of Dylan, Joan Baez, and Paul Simon and, in Britain, of Donovan, Al Stewart, and many others, expressed a new feeling, a new philosophy. Cannabis, as a new pleasure-giving drug which many claimed was an aid to self-awareness, increased in popularity within a scene which emphasized self-awareness and the individual and rejected the tired conventions of a society geared to violence and destruction. Paul Simon sang:[13]

> Blessed is the land and the kingdom,
> Blessed is the man whose soul belongs to,
> Blessed are the meth drinkers,
>   pot sellers,
>   illusion dwellers.
> O Lord, why have you forsaken me?

By 1965 cannabis was significantly affecting large numbers of urban working-class teenagers in London and other cities. But the spread through the social and class divisions meant that it was no longer possible to associate cannabis use with any characteristic philosophy or way of life, any artistic or musical preferences, any political outlook. The old traditions within the "pot" scene have in many cases remained, but the former value of the drug as a symbol of the identity of a particular group was now obsolete. "We're all smokers now" might summarize the change by which cannabis smoking spread to the working-class adolescent culture of most British cities and towns. The typical cannabis user therefore does not exist. Moreover, there is little in common between the middle-class hippy "pot"-smoker in Notting Hill Gate and the working-class delinquent in the East End. Some would claim that cannabis has helped to break down class divisions: the same claim has been made for alcohol, Freemasonry, homosexuality, and war. As far as cannabis is concerned, there is little evidence of the truth of this claim. On the contrary, there are clear class structures within the drug scene, the connoisseurs despising the naive experimenters, the "acid-heads" despising those who are still at the "pot" level, hippies treating the working-class "pillhead" with contempt, and so on.

Goode, who studied multiple drug use among cannabis users in the United States, emphasized that those areas where the cannabis-LSD connection is strong are precisely those where the cannabis-heroin connection is weak. He showed that there was not a single cannabis subculture but several and describes three patterns, each of which involved cannabis misuse, but which were fundamentally different. The narcotics cycle involved the street addict, and it was in this context, the slum ghetto zone, that the link between cannabis and heroin was strong. The amphetamine cycle involved mainly white, lower middle-class teenagers, and the association here was principally between cannabis and amphetamines. The psychedelic cycle was more "sophisticated", involved the use of cannabis and other hallucinogens, and was more clearly a proselytizing group.

The British experience suggests a similar pattern. The junkie subculture was, until two or three years ago, predominantly middle class, and here cannabis and heroin use were closely associated. Today there are more working-class addicts. The "pot and pill" cycle, however, is numerically much stronger and involves a large number of working-class delinquents, with little or no involvement in the heroin scene. The hippy world, in which cannabis figures prominently, is far removed in every respect from urban working-class delinquent society. In one area of East London with a high delinquency ratio, the occasional visits of long-haired youths in hippy gear are greeted with shouts of derision and contempt by the drug-using adolescent community.

Cannabis is a pleasure-giving drug, and the element of sheer pleasure and enjoyment is fundamental. In many cases it is used as an alternative to alcohol by young people who are virtually teetotal, while in others the use of both drugs is conventional and common. It is mistaken to assume that the cannabis-user is necessarily trying to "escape" from his problems. This seems the least satisfactory explanation of all. As one smoker has pointed out:[14]

It has often been asserted that drug use of any kind is a form of escapism and should be strongly discouraged on that ground alone.... But I have gained the impression that cannabis is a poor escape route. Alcohol may blot out reality, but cannabis tends to magnify it. If one turns on when one is feeling bad, cannabis usually has the effect of making one feel miserable. The sort of person who wants to escape from reality may turn to heroin or they may turn to the Church, but they are unlikely to continue to smoke cannabis.

2. THE PILL SCENE: THE SOHO PATTERN

Witnesses have told us that there are numerous clubs, many in the West End of London, enjoying a vogue among young people who can find in them such diversions as modern music and all-night dancing.

Drug Addiction, Second Report of the Interdepartmental Committee, 1965[15]

For some years amphetamine misuse was synonymous with the Soho scene which remains a strategic point for the present traffic. Some understanding of Soho is important in understanding the drug scene, for at a number of points the club life of the West End of London affects the young "pep pill" experimenter, even if it is only at the level of the casual visit or absorption of facets of Soho life gleaned from the press. In some ways Soho is the archetype of pill scenes everywhere. In others it is untypical, for it contains deviant groups, subcultures of very disturbed young people who are the rejects of other towns and cities, the very badly damaged casualties of other districts. As one psychiatrist observed after a visit in 1966, "The majority are badly damaged by the time they get to Soho, they are not attractive propositions to anyone, and I do not know how they should be dealt with."[16]

Soho is the district of West London which is roughly bounded by Leicester Square and Coventry Street to the south, Regent Street to the West, Oxford Street to the north, and Charing Cross Road to the East. It contains a few thousand permanent residents, and a heavy concentration of theatres, cinemas, coffee bars, restaurants, strip clubs, and shops displaying "Books". Within Soho, a complex of worlds exist, with little contact with each other: theatrical people, workers in the record and film industries, addicts, "normal" and homosexual prostitutes, the coffee club clientèle, alcoholics, and young drifters, as well as the large number who simply visit the West End occasionally for eating and drinking parties. The statue of Eros symbolically stands at the south-western boundary, and Soho might fittingly be termed an "erogenous zone".

Although national attention did not focus on the amphetamine traffic in Soho until 1963, there is no doubt that there was a pill scene in the early 1950s. However, 1963–5 was the crucial period for the structuring of the amphetamine market within a clearly defined geographical area. Most of the young people who are now to be found within the coffee clubs and coffee bars are aged between 17 and 20. Of 150 young drug-takers who were helped at St Anne's Soho in 1968, only two were aged under 16, while 64 were aged 17–20, 46 were 21–25, and 38 were over 25.[17] In the general circle of young people within the Soho pill scene, two categories could be easily differentiated. First, the "weekenders" who used mostly the large, well-advertised beat, rhythm-and-blues, soul and folk clubs, but also were involved on the fringe of the pill scene in the smaller all-night clubs. Secondly, the "hard core" of the very disturbed who belonged, if they belonged anywhere, to the twilight world of Soho. Many of these were well known in the prisons and borstals, and some had long histories of being in care, in approved schools, and so on.

With its characteristic combination of naivety and archaic English, the Brain Report of 1965 revealed its discovery that there existed "numerous clubs" which were currently "enjoying a vogue", and where young people could find "diversions" such as modern music and all-night dancing.[18] In fact, since this period, there has been a marked decline in the role played by the West End in relation to the large numbers of working-class, delinquent drug-takers who once provided a sizeable proportion of its weekend clientèle. More and more young people are turning to less tired and more exciting scenes in other parts of London. One close observer within the youth service commented in 1969:[19]

> Since 1963–4, the time of The Discothèque in Wardour Street and the rush of clubs run by Nash; the time of pep-pill parties in the Leicester Square conveniences—when for a moment innocent girls and boys felt they had latched on to something really *new*—the word has come back—the West End's had it. Certainly the action in the last two or three years has been much more on the perimeter of London: a whole club-going sector of the youth of Inner London turned their backs on the pathetic con of Soho and the West End, and it's doubtful if they will ever need to come back.

On the other hand, the "hard core" of the "pillhead" group in Soho has remained. Until about 1966 it was possible to divide Soho, drugwise, into the "junkie" scene at the Piccadilly end, and the "pillhead" scene north of Shaftesbury Avenue. There was little contact between the two groups. The pill scene was a fairly conservative one, the substances involved being almost entirely Dexedrine, Drinamyl, Durophet, and to a lesser degree Preludin. But from 1966 onwards there was an ominous change in the structure of the amphetamine market, brought about by the spread of intravenous methylamphetamine, usually in the form of Methedrine. This epidemic reached its peak in 1968, and could be traced largely to the surgeries of two general practitioners. Methylamphetamine brought the "junkies" and "pillheads" closer together, but it also brought into existence a new type of intravenous drug-taker, the "meth-freak". The use of Methylamphetamine, known as "speed", had been for some years a common feature of young pill scenes and of hippy scenes in the United States, where the drug is sometimes used as a sexual stimulant ("balling speed", a process of absorbing methylamphetamine through the genital mucosa[20] or combined with heroin and a barbiturate in the same injection, "bombita").[21] In London the "meth" epidemic involved heroin addicts—88 per cent of

D'Orbans group of heroin addicts used methylamphetamine with heroin,[22] while 86 per cent of Hawks' sample of methylamphetamine users had used heroin[23]—and also a significant number who had progressed from *oral* to *intravenous* use of amphetamines. Some of these, after the restrictions on methylamphetamine in October 1968, changed either to heroin or to methadone.

In Soho many young amphetamine users show clear signs of psycho-sexual disturbance. The overlap between the "pill" scene and the "gay" (homosexual) scene is significant but at certain points misleading. The homosexual world is different from the world of the drug user. Within the "gay" scene, there are divisions based on age, class, and so on. The very respectable "gay" clubs, the more sleazy drinking bars and pick-up points, the adolescent coffee-clubs, the young "dilly boys" (male prostitutes)—these represent different, but at certain points overlapping, communities within the homosexual world. The last two groups are the most likely to be involved in drug use, since they involve more adolescents who are still uncertain of their sexual orientation. Nobody working in Soho can hope to understand the problems of amphetamine misuse who does not understand something of the problems of the young homosexual.

Soho collects damaged elements from other districts. In this respect it represents a microcosm not of the drug scene as a whole but of the more disturbed elements within it. The young amphetamine user is frequently more disturbed, more difficult to help, and more rootless than the heroin addict. In the Soho club scene he finds some sense of belonging.

3. THE LONDON SCENE AND THE REST OF BRITAIN

... the social geography of London shows some signs of a drawing together—the broad divisions are less striking than they were twenty or even ten years ago. And yet there are

also contrary signs of moving apart—of a new kind of diversi-
fication, which may well be equally, if not more significant.
                                                    MRS RUTH GLASS[2]

Those who view the drug scene from outside may identify
it, quite mistakenly, as a monolithic structure. In reality,
it presents a pattern of contradictions, holding within it
class, social and cultural divergence, some of which are
narrowed, others widened, and it holds within it a variety
of subcultural worlds which often have less in common
with each other than the "straight" observer might imagine.
In addition, it is misleading to view this complex wholly
from the angle of drug abuse, since some of these subcultures are held together by more fundamental and positive
bonds than pharmacological ones. To summarize the
various groups involved in drug abuse is to see how varie-
gated the pattern is, and what is said of London, could,
with qualifications, be applied to the national scene.

First, there is the *student drug scene*. The drugs used by
students are generally cannabis or amphetamines and, apart
from the ever-present minority of drug connoisseurs, the
actual knowledge of drugs is superficial. The young delinquent "hash"-sellers in Liverpool 8, for instance, treat the
students with contempt and see them as fair game for the
sale of "bad" cannabis. Only rarely does one encounter
serious problems of physical addiction among students.
Binnie, in a study in a provincial university,[25] reported that,
of a sample of 2424 students, 228 (9·44 per cent) had used
some drugs, but most (84 per cent) of these had restricted
themselves to cannabis and amphetamines. Only 5 per cent
of the drug users (0·6 per cent of the total) had used opiates,
and 11 per cent of the users (1 per cent of the total) had
used LSD.

Secondly, there is the *beatnik scene*. The "old-fashioned"
beats of the late 1950s and early 1960s, described by Sally
Trench in her *Bury Me In My Boots*,[26] came on to the
London scene at the beginning of the Campaign for

Nuclear Disarmament. They went "on the road" but sub-sequently returned to Trafalgar Square which is their habitat. This older tradition of beatniks was self-consciously anti-establishment and at some points it represented the relics of a disillusioned Left. Sally Trench divided the beats into three types: the permanent beats, who never moved far from Trafalgar Square, the "homing" beats, who went off "on the road" for periods but always returned, and the wandering beats, who never stayed in the same place for long.[27]

The old beatnik community has now virtually dis-integrated. But a new type of beat, the "Piccadilly beat", is emerging into consciousness, and strictly belongs to the Underground scene. These see the role of the beats in relation to the authoritarian power-structure, and they articulate their discontent in terms which show the in-fluence of the revolutionary student movement. As with the old beats, the degree of drug involvement may be con-siderable, but it is not the most significant feature of this community. The "Commune of the Streets", a beat soli-darity group created to resist police "harassment" around Piccadilly Circus, express the position of the beats in rela-tion to the other scenes in this way:[28]

> Apart from the junkie scene, there is also the gay scene, and the buskers form a third independent grouping. And in addition there is the beats, or drop-outs, our scene, which overlaps the other three but which cannot be reduced to them, and which has its own distinctive features. There are beats who hustle, or who push, or fix. There are also beats who are on the lookout for sugar daddies, and beats who busk to get bread. What distinguishes us as beats and drop-outs, from the other groups is that, unlike them, we don't define our presence on the street exclusively in terms of any of these activities, but in terms of a general opposition *vis-à-vis* straight society.

This group is beginning to think in terms of training "anti-social workers" from within the scene and attempting self-help and welfare. In 1969 they "occupied" various properties in the West End, which attracted considerable press publicity.

The third important group is the "young drifters". This term has almost become a youth work cliché, and it may therefore be forgotten that many of those categorized as "drifters" not only do not "drift" very far, but also belong to other scenes and groups. The "young drifters" differ from the classical vagrants in age, and from the beats in their degree of self-consciousness. They belong to the world of "new-style vagrants" whose "problem is socio-clinical rather than economic".[29] They are rootless, often very inadequate or psychopathic, and they constitute an increasing group within the London scene. Some of them are addicts, some are "pill-heads", some are homosexual, but it is their rootlessness which characterizes them above all else. One youth project in West London was in touch with 90 such young people in 1966. 19 per cent came from the north-west and 27 per cent from the home counties. 87 per cent came from highly industrialized urban areas. 78 per cent were homeless and destitute when they were contacted in London. Half of them did not come from "broken homes" but 41 per cent had been deprived of one or both parents, including 19 per cent deprived of their father. Drugs played a prominent role: 69 per cent had used drugs—33 per cent amphetamines, 22 per cent cannabis, and 11 per cent heroin.[30] The use of amphetamines was most popular since it provided a positive prop for their way of life, and enabled them to stay awake for long hours without food.

More detailed information about these young drifters emerges from a survey of 102 young people at a well known drifters' club run by the Salvation Army in West London.[31] The mean age of those interviewed was 22·08, the largest single groups being aged 18 and 21. Their places of origin were as follows: Greater London, 26; Liverpool and Manchester, 11; other parts of England, 18; Glasgow, 13; other parts of Scotland, 10; Dublin, 7; Eire, 11; Northern Ireland,

6

3. (See also I. P. James' figures for places and ages of 100 heroin addicts below). 51 per cent showed evidence of disturbed family background. 25 had been "on the road" between two and three years, and 23 over six years, while 72 were currently "on the road". About half did casual work only. 34 slept regularly in facilities provided at a West End church, 15 in derelict houses, 20 in friends' flats, and 25 in their own flats. Only 4 had eaten over four meals during the previous 24 hours, while 12 had had three meals, 10 had had one snack, and 10 had had no food at all. Their current pattern of drug use was not unlike that reported above: 27 used cannabis, 15 heroin, 12 methylamphetamine, 15 methadone (Physeptone), 17 amphetamines, and 7 other "pills". 46 had been in prison or borstal.

Within the drug scene, the "young drifters" are more akin to the amphetamine culture than to the opiate addicts. But the scenes fade into each other, and it is confusing to categorize them solely in terms of substances used. Some of the drifters lack the stability to become heroin addicts, for their inability to follow a settled way of life applies as much to the regular routine of the addict's day as to any other clock-geared pattern. Like the methylamphetamine users, they will move from one drug to another with surprising speed, and they are as unstable in their drug use as in their whole lives.

Fourthly, there is the *pillhead scene*. The study of methylamphetamine users mentioned above revealed striking similarities at some points to the studies of young drifters. For instance, just under half had suffered parental bereavement or separation before the age of 16. 30 per cent had eaten only occasional snacks in the last few days. 68 per cent had slept rough at some time and 19 per cent were of no fixed abode. 32 per cent had been in prison, borstal, or other penal institutions. Of this group, however, 86 per cent had used heroin, and there were high percentages for other drugs used: 91 per cent cannabis, 73 per cent for amphetamine, 88 per cent for amphetamine-barbiturate compounds. (The mean age of first use of amphetamines was 16·88, and that of amphetamine-barbiturates was 16·96, while that of first use of cannabis was 17·16.)[32]

But, as has been shown, the "meth" user represents a particular type of development with roots in both "pill-head" and "junkie" scenes. The majority of amphetamine users have remained *oral* users. In London the "pill" scene is different from the world of the "young drifter". The typical pill-user will be a working-class delinquent or fringe delinquent, usually from one of the London boroughs or from an adjoining county. He probably works, and his life-style is that of the conventional delinquent.

In Soho, he visits the all-night clubs and bars, perhaps only at weekends. Money is an important element in his life, and he will be more interested in clothes and conservative in his adherence to current fashions and *mores*. He will be conservative, too, in his drug use, which will be largely restricted to Drinamyl, Dexedrine, and cannabis. He will view the more deviant groups as "weirdies" and will be inclined to treat them with a lack of sympathy, if not active hostility. He conforms to the pattern of the classical "juvenile delinquent", and his amphetamine misuse is simply the most recent addition to his delinquent activities.

Fifthly, there is the *junkie scene*. Chein and his colleagues observed, in passing, that British heroin addicts were mainly middle class, geographically dispersed, and rarely in contact with each other.[33] Since then the pattern of heroin abuse has become more complex. There are now significant groups of working-class delinquents in both old and new urban areas, and of vagrant, "drifting", quasi-beats, within the heroin scene.[34] A good example of the working-class delinquent addict scene is Stepney in East London. Here one sees a young person, living at home, with a history of educational failures and, in most cases, of delinquent activity. The mother usually dominates the family set-up, the father being virtually non-existent. At the treatment centre which serves this district, 50 per cent of the patients are in full-time employment, while "the larger number within the unemployed group are from outside the immediate area and are unemployable".[35] These addicts are not *au fait* with the folk-art-jazz syndrome of the West End, nor do they relate at any point to the beatnik pattern.

The vagrant, "drifting" addict is a familiar figure around Piccadilly Circus, and has been labelled the "Piccadilly junkie". There was a period not long ago when Piccadilly played both an economic and a symbolic role in the heroin scene, and was therefore used by very large numbers of addicts. The economic role lay in the presence of the all-night chemist, use of which was necessary in the days when addicts handled their weeks' prescriptions. Since the Dangerous Drugs Act 1967, prescriptions have been posted to the chemist nearest to the addict's normal place of abode. Consequently, the remaining "Piccadilly junkies" are those who are homeless and who form a sub-group within the "young drifter" scene. Piccadilly survives only as a symbolic point, a kind of junkie Mecca, and a "fixing" point for the homeless. An increasing number of these drifting addicts are girls. In D'Orban's prison study, 53 per cent of the addicts were of no fixed abode.

Although the word "junkie" has historically been equated with "heroin addict" it is becoming impossible to limit it in this way. The increase in methadone (Physeptone) abuse has brought a new and disturbing factor into the junkie scene. Physeptone is generally seen as a "withdrawal drug" and a narcotic antagonist. But the whole basis of the Dole-Nyswander "methadone maintenance" programme in the United States is the fact that the patient reports to the clinic daily and receives his supply (orally) on the spot. The prescribing to addicts of large amounts of injectible Physeptone is not in any sense what the Dole-Nyswander plan envisaged, and it has created a crop of Physeptone addicts, not all of whom were formerly on heroin. A study of 100 addicts in prison in 1969 showed that, of 60 who were being supplied by clinics, 51 were receiving Physeptone and 35 heroine and that, of 27 whose sources of supply were entirely illicit, 13 were obtaining Physeptone and 26 heroin. Only 13 were receiving Physeptone from general practitioners, including five from the same doctor.[37] The increase in Physeptone addicts is a clinic-induced pheno- menon. The figures, however, obscure the crucial difference between the use of oral Physeptone (tablets or linctus) and of injectible Physeptone (ampoules). To substitute injec- tion of Physeptone for injection of heroin does not weaken the addiction to the needle and merely changes the structure of the junkie subculture while perpetuating and indeed strengthening it. Moreover, since few addict clinics in Britain open on Saturday and none on Sunday, the opera- tion of the Dole-Nyswander "methadone maintenance" programme in the form in which it was intended is im- possible.

Increasingly, then, one must include the Physeptone addict within the "Piccadilly junkie" scene. Where do the London addicts come from? The above-mentioned prison study showed the places of origin of 100 male addicts as follows: London, 25; Home Counties, 11; rest of England, 23; Wales, 1; Northern Ireland, 0; Scotland, 15; Eire, 17; Australia, 1; New Zealand, 1; Cyprus, 1; Jamaica, 1; France, 1; Holland, 1; United States, 1; Persia, 1.[38] Comparison with the Salvation Army report cited above shows roughly the same distribution pattern with the marked prominence of London, Scotland, and Eire. Looked at from one point of view, the young vagrant, whether addict or not, repre- sents a particular facet of the "drift to the south", the economic migration from the depressed, underdeveloped areas to the metropolis.

Finally, in London, there is the *hippy scene*. If Soho may be seen as a pillhead zone, and Piccadilly as the junkies' focal point, it is Notting Hill, "Scene W.11", which has become the geographical base of the Underground. Seen in terms of drug use, it is a "pot" and "acid" scene, but to view the Underground solely, or principally, from a drug angle is to misunderstand its significance. More than any other section of the London scene, the Underground is primarily an attempt to create a new society. The American Underground was well-established by the end of 1966, and its British counterpart was emerging. Caroline Coon, who founded Release as the hippy legal advice and welfare service, sees the emergence of the Underground as that of a "new type of self-conception".

> We believe that the hippy should be seen as a product of a society whose moral spirit is lower and more disillusioned than it has been for a long time. Our reaction has been a desire to create a group with a mode of living which is a conscientiously cultivated work of art.[39]

On this view, recreation and play (*homo ludens* as the prototype of the hippy) are central characteristics of the new society which the hippy wishes to construct. "Dropping-out" and drug use are important because they contradict the values of "straight" society, based on the dominant role of the occupation for the male, and the emphasis on planning for the future. By contrast, the hippy emphasizes self-expression, play, and the enhancement of the present, a process aided by cannabis.

The authentic hippy is non-violent and sets a high value on gentleness and the rejection of anger (though his aggression is often seen in attitudes of cynicism, contempt for "straight" society, and psychedelic superiority). "Do your own thing" involves respect for individuality, and rejects attempts to force conformity. He emphasizes the need for intimacy in sexual and emotional relationships and he has a strong sense of group spirit. He rejects straight society and its educational, religious, and political institutions. His sense of the "mystical" varies. Indeed, one American study suggests that the healthy hippies stress brotherhood and group solidarity, whereas it is the sick, border-line, psychotic hippies who show "mystic" traits combined with considerable chronic depression.[40]

In Britain the summer of 1967 was the crucial period for the flowering of the hippy scene. The term "flower people" had been coined by a Californian disc-jockey promoting a rock group called The Seeds[41] and, during the summer of 1967, when beautiful people wearing beads and bells began to appear in London streets, "flower power" came to symbolize the gentleness and peace which, in theory at least, characterized the hippy scene. Scott MacKenzie's record "San Francisco", with its tale of "gentle people with flowers in their hair", was on every juke-box and played a very important role in fostering the hippy ethos. That beautiful summer quickly faded, and is still yearned for somewhat nostalgically by those who were around the West End then. Since then the glory has departed. One Underground "mystical scene magazine" lamented:[42]

Whatever happened to the magic of psychedelic summers past when we could walk out in the streets and know that anyone with hair and timeless garb was one of ourselves in the evolving Brotherhood of the Spirit? Time was when a friend was anyone who caught our eye as they passed, in the joyous recognition of each other as fellow conspirators of Love.... But since hip gear and hairstyles have become the "in-thing" nowadays, it's hard to tell a Brother of the Spirit from a "plastic hippie" until you try to greet him.

Much of the early idealism and genuine spirituality of the hippy scene has now disintegrated. "Plastic hippies" are everywhere but, as with so many other "religious" sects, the inner spirit has faded. A psychologist whose field of activity is the hippy community in Berkeley has written of "psychedelic hypocrisy",[43] while in Britain a well-known Underground worker has warned that the scene has developed its own Establishment:[44]

A year of exposure to the problems arising out of the "alternative society", through working at BIT, showed me above all that the new generation, with its philosophy of love, and its rejection of secondhand material values, is in fact just as lost and confused as any preceding generation. The flowers and beads and gentle exterior is, for the individual, just as much a straight-jacket as the uniforms and guns and marching feet of the generation before.

The complaint that the hippy scene has become superficial and phoney is a constantly recurring one, and it comes from different quarters. Thus from East London comes a protest against the class nature of the Underground:[45]

Yes, I really get mad on with these big-hearted underground snobs. I call them the hippie-flippie-groovy people. Last summer when it began to happen was beautiful. But now it's so plastic, with all this look at me I'm the happiest man in the world bit and a bread scene even. Once I got involved in a discussion with some of these cats—soon as I opened my mouth everyone looked. God, when will the plastic underground forgive me for my Bethnal Green accent.

The class nature of the Underground has been eroded to some degree by the spread of new musical techniques: "acid rock", with its combination of electronically produced rock'n roll-type sounds and surrealist images, and the profound impact of musical "drugless trips",—exciting and important musical patterns of which the Beatles', the Fugs', and the Byrds' work are key examples. What is termed "Underground music" is characterized by strangeness, abstraction, unworldliness, and love of natural things. Jethro Tull and the Incredible String Band are clear instances, while the Pentangle, Tyrannosaurus Rex, Dylan, and contemporary folk groups such as Simon and Garfunkel in the United States and Magna Carta in Britain stand at the point of intersection of the Underground and the progressive folk traditions. The development of these new musical patterns should be seen in close relation to the spread of an Underground culture. It is only against this kind of positive background that the hippy drug scene should be viewed.

The hippy scene is mainly a "pot" and "acid" scene. Although in the American hippy communities methylamphetamine abuse has reached major proportions,[46] in Britain the responsible voices within the Underground preached the message "Speed Kills" and this, advertised in *International Times* and disseminated at Middle Earth and other clubs, reduced the amount of amphetamine abuse within the hippy communities. Indeed the class division mentioned above does, to some degree, correlate with drug use, since the articulate, middle-class hippies who use cannabis and LSD are set over against the inarticulate working class, possibly delinquent, amphetamine-users. The types of drug abuse most commonly found on the Underground scene are probably those associated with "potheads" who have ceased to be productive and sit around all day having ideas which are never fulfilled: and those associated with "bad trips", the psychotic episodes described earlier in discussing LSD. One writer has, however commented:[48]

> This aspect of the Underground has received undesirable notoriety, ironically giving the movement more impetus, but in themselves drugs are becoming less of an issue, except legally, nor are they a serious medical problem.

The patterns of drug abuse within the London scene are, in many ways, a microcosm of the country as a whole. Two facts emerge from this discussion. First, that there are diverse and distinct "drug scenes" involving different substances and affecting different social groups. Secondly, that "drug scenes" are themselves elements of other scenes, some of the positive, as well as the destructive, features of which have been outlined.

7

Pastoral Care
and the Drug Scene

1. THE CHURCH AT THE SCENE OF CRISIS

> Thus said the Lord my God: "Become shepherd of the
> flock doomed to slaughter.... So I became the shepherd of
> the flock doomed to be slain for those who trafficked in the
> sheep.... And I tended the sheep.   *Zechariah 2.4, 7*

> It's a long road to Canaan
> On Bleecker Street.   PAUL SIMON[1]

Pastoral care of the drug taker may involve churches at one
of two levels. The first is that of the area of infection, in
which the church is situated in an inner-city district where
drug abuse is common. One might term this type of care
"casualty caring". The second, which affects far more
churches numerically, is the "long-term caring" for young
drug takers, addicts, or ex-addicts within their home community or within a new environment. The casualty type of
work will be discussed first. In both, one needs to emphasize
that the Church's concern is with *healing*, not in the strict
medical sense of the abolition of symptoms by treating or
modifying the cause which produced them, but in the older
sense of the formation of a new condition, the birth of a
new creation. Salvation, in biblical thought, is not a soli-
tary, individualist concept, but a corporate one, for it involves the "making whole" of the community, "the healing
of the nations" (Rev. 22.2). So the Church in its pastoral
care is not simply concerned with the counselling and

guidance of individuals, but primarily with the building up of the body of Christ (Eph. 4.12). Too much emphasis has been placed, within the current "pastoral care" movements, on a clinical model, which sees "sickness" as a private disturbance, and shows little understanding of the social forces and the community structure. This has been particularly so in the case of drug addicts, where many Christians have tended to see the "drug subculture" as wholly evil, and have regarded the extrication of the addict from his environment as the fundamental prerequisite of "rehabilitation". Theologically this view is based on protestant individualistic concepts, and pays little attention to the healing of the "drug subculture" as such.

The theological principle behind the Church's involvement in the inner-city crisis districts is that the drug-taking subcultures can only be truly redeemed from within. The Church's role therefore is not to rescue and isolate individual members (though it should be emphasized that this is often a necessary stage in healing), but to build within the subcultural groups the structures of spiritual renewal. This is the pattern of Incarnation, the self-annihilation of God within the suffering of humanity: only when the grain of wheat dies into the earth does resurrection become possible (John 12.24). The central task then is the creation of a community in which if one member suffers all suffer (1 Cor. 12.26), a community characterized by the sharing of bread and of all life (Acts 2.42, 44), and this creation is the work of the Spirit, using the members of the body.

In some ways to achieve a sense of "common life" within the drug scene is easier than in conventional communities, for so often one finds those who share a common sense of rejection and isolation will create among themselves a society where the isolation, suffering, and personal misery are shared. The sympathy, understanding, and compassion within drug scenes frequently puts Christian communities to shame. In fact it is probable that the growth of drug scenes is "an unconscious rebellion against ... disengagement of the brother with brother",[2] a protest against the increasing dehumanization of the technocratic age. To such an age the addictive state represents a desperate cry for help. In the words of one ex-addict:

> It's sad that they have to go this far to get help. I think "help" is what they want rather than attention. After all, if you wear weird enough clothes you'll get attention. I used to want help but I couldn't say so. I only got it when I became a junkie.

In districts like Soho, the cry for help, for love, for acceptance, comes pathetically and powerfully not only from addicts but from a large number of rootless, unhappy, lonely people.

There is an important difference between the Soho adolescent scene and that in many other inner-city districts. In Soho, which is not a major residential district, young people often only appear as part of a drug scene or disturbed group after a certain "danger point" has been passed. By the time they arrive in the West End they are badly damaged. The residential districts of other cities and towns, as well as of London, therefore present more perplexing problems to the Church and other caring groups, problems involving preventive work, actions which might avoid the crises occuring. One fact which emerges from talking to young people in the Soho clubs is the need that many of them felt to discuss and "talk through" their emotional, sexual, spiritual problems with someone in their home area, but could find no one. Sadly their picture of the clergy is not impressive: they report with depressing frequency, that "you couldn't talk to him", that he represented the boring, respectable, "square" world from which they were trying to escape. Similarly, the Church as a community seemed to epitomize all that was unsatisfactory in society: its complacency, half-heartedness, compromise, lukewarmness, and general unawareness of "where it's at". A happier picture emerges where priests have made their homes, as well as the Church, into centres of hospitality, where youngsters could be accepted for what they were (not as potential "pew-fodder") and could talk freely without inhibitions. The degree to which a cup of coffee, a record-player, and a non-patronizing approach can break down barriers and fears is difficult to exaggerate. Again, in many districts a particular café, coffee bar, or club provides the gathering point for the local "problem kids". A priest who, without ostentation or the pathetic, assumed "with-it" facade which every teenager sees through at once, would make a point of "being around" regularly, simply to drink coffee and talk, would be accomplishing more in the building up of trust than any "results" might show. Where there are detached youth workers and coffee bar "projects" in the neighbourhood, a close liaison between the priest and the local youth worker is indispensable.

The need for "street work" is clearly shown in many "crisis districts" as well as ordinary residential neighbourhoods. The work done by such youth workers as Paddy McCarthy and Geoff Bevan in Notting Hill, Barbara Ward in Soho, or Barrie Biven in Hoxton has suggested that the young delinquent or fringe-delinquent may often be helped by a "floating" or detached youth worker, perhaps based on a café, but moving around, making contacts at street level. Work at St Ann's Soho, has certainly indicated that there is a role which could be played by the "detached priest", detached, not in the sense that he is unconnected with the local cell of the Body of Christ, but in the sense that he is uncommitted to a parochial, institutional set-up, which is as often an obstacle to the Body of Christ as it is to the young people on the street.

In Britain, as in the Ramirez Programme in New York,[3] contact with the addict in the street may be the initial stage in "treatment". Certainly, in Soho, it has been found that certain initial contacts, often in the middle of the night, can be crucial, but there needs then to be intensive follow-up and care *within* the area of infection often for a very considerable period. During this period, contacts with the medical service in prisons and borstals, and with the psychiatrist, nurses, and social workers at hospitals are of great importance. The work of the Salvation Army youth workers at the Rink Club in London is an excellent example of pastoral care within the framework of the "drifter" subculture. Using the crypt of a church as a contact point and a day-time sleeping centre, the Rink workers have built up within the West End scene the beginnings of a caring community, committed to the love of their brothers, which might ultimately destroy the alienation and hopelessness of the drifter's life.

The nature of pastoral care *within* the drug subculture is also brought out clearly by considering the position of the Simon Community. Formed as a confederation of local communities in 1963, Simon has some thirteen projects throughout the country. Its concern is with social inadequacy in general but, as well as attempting long-term care and treatment, Simon workers operate at "Skid Row" level, with vagrant alcoholics and methylated spirit drinkers, and have a close contact with the drifting young addict.

> Simon does not seek to rehabilitate but to *contain*. Its aim is to accept, assimilate, and then sort out ... Simon workers, however, should not fall into the trap of *aiming* to restore to an unsympathetic society the men and women who, over and over again, have failed most, if not all, formal attempts to cure them.[4]

Simon workers aim to eradicate the "we and they" concept in social work, and their houses are non-institutional. Houses of hospitality, night shelters in which the kitchen is the focal point, usually take some eight residents with four workers and four emergency "one-night-stands", while there are other houses, usually outside the inner-city areas, where there is less pressure and more room for individual help. What is crucial about Simon, and indeed about the other groups operating in "areas of infection", is that their pastoral care functions *within* the framework of alienation:

... to some extent we are working at a "failure level" and it would be unrealistic to aim (as do most social workers) for rehabilitation, reform or cure.[5]

This kind of ministry is so unfamiliar to many people that it needs emphasis. It is a ministry in which the suffering and hopelessness is not so much removed as absorbed, taken into the Body of Christ and shared, with no ulterior motives and no *a priori* assumption that one's efforts will result in "reform" or "rehabilitation". It is a ministry which

underlines the fact that the church must suffer and be crucified with those it seeks to serve: and that it must keep on being crucified even though the nails bite deep and the hope of resurrection is obscure.[6]

Turning specifically to drugs, there are three sets of facts which those who work within drug scenes will need to know: how to recognize signs of drug use and danger signs; whom to contact for further help; and what to do in cases of overdose or "bad trips".

(a) Signs of Drug Use and Danger Signs

Many of the "signs" circulated to schools and youth clubs are not particularly helpful, since the indications of drug misuse or abuse frequently are hard to distinguish from common adolescent mood disturbances. The worker who becomes sensitive to the scene will soon begin to recognize signs of deterioration or of chronic abuse of a substance. What follows needs to be read with commonsense and seen against the background of what has been written about the drugs in Part One.

Cannabis has a quite distinctive smell, rather like burning sage. Signs of cannabis use may include slow slurred speech, excitability and inane laughter, fatuous, dreamy expression, flushed face, relaxed but unsteady walk, lack of interest in what is going on around, and wide glazed eyes. Brown stains on the fingers, increased hunger and thirst with a preference for sweet food and drinks, dry cough, and reddening of the eyes may be noticed. Indications that the cannabis user is deteriorating may include: difficulties in concentration; failing memory; decrease in mathematical ability; a kind of "creeping paranoia" with ideas of persecution; exaggerated feelings either of self-confidence or inferiority; passivity, loss of energy and desire; difficulty in articulating thoughts and in expression; increasing "hang-ups" in close relationships especially with parents and with girl friends or boy friends; increased impulsiveness and tendency to "fly off the handle"; a sense of futility and hopelessness about the future; and an emphatic and total denial that cannabis is in any sense harmful.

The signs of *amphetamine* abuse have been discussed earlier, but they may include: restlessness and irritable behaviour; alternating moods of elation and depression; a "bright-eyed" look combined with a lack of tact; photophobia (fear of bright lights which hurt the eyes) and large pupils which may lead to the wearing of dark glasses; loss of appetite and weight, but increased thirst, dry mouth, and bad breath; a tendency to sleep late on Mondays and to stay out all night.

With the abuse of *opiates*, the indications are more apparent.[7] Changes in behaviour may be associated with a recent "fix", or a "come down", or with the addict's way of life, and may include such signs as the following:

(i) *Changes in behaviour associated with a recent "fix"*: Small pin-point pupils; dreamy, detached look; fresh injection marks; loss of appetite or interest in food; rubbing of eyes, chin, and nose and scratching of arms and legs; speech slow and slurred; resentfulness of being disturbed and of noise and bright lights; wakefulness interrupted by drowsiness; eyes wide open but glazed, red, and puffy; relaxed posture; constant examination of arms; frequent visits to the lavatory; inability to concentrate.

(ii) *Changes in behaviour associated with "come down"*: Irritability and wanting to be left alone; fidgeting with hands, pacing up and down; inability to concentrate; perspiration; loss of appetite; yawning; running eyes and nose; heavy smoking.

(iii) *Changes in behaviour associated with addict's way of life:* Blood spots on clothes, especially pyjama tops and shirts; unexpected absence from home; sleeping out; increased number of telephone calls and new visitors at home; abandonment of organized activities; poor appetite; slow, halting speech; loss of interest in personal appearance; stooped posture; long periods spent alone; fully burnt matches found lying around; litter in room and pockets.

Some of these signs, of course, are more likely to be noticed by parents, but awareness of their significance will help those in a position to give advice, or to take action at the critical moment.

(b) Whom to Contact for Further Help

A list of addresses is given in Appendix 1. It is very important for clergy and social workers in "areas of infection" to be in close touch with the local treatment centre. Incalculable harm has been done by well-intentioned "do-gooders" who attempt to work apart from the statutory agencies or even apart from other groups within the same scene. Such behaviour is not only impractical and wasteful, but it can do considerable damage to young people, who find themselves pulled in different directions by different groups. In the development of pastoral care within a community, close liaison between priest, psychiatrist, social worker, youth leader, probation officer, and so on is invaluable. In some districts, a loose structured "consortium" of those within the immediate area involved with young drug-takers can be of tremendous value in the prevention of unnecessary overlap and in the sharing of common problems. One of the most useful pieces of work which such a group can do is to build up a card-index of people within the area to whom particular types of problem can be referred, places where emergency or long term accommodation is available, and so on.

In general the local "treatment centres" are concerned only with heroin addicts, but many young heroin users probably ought rather to be referred for help to an outpatient psychiatric clinic. This applies even more to "pill-heads" and chronic cannabis users, where the underlying psychological disturbances are invariably more important than the drug used. Individual psychotherapy may be suitable in some cases, but many of the problems encountered among young drug takers are best dealt with by youth workers, clergy, or social workers within the natural environment. The moment one introduces a psychiatrist from an alien world there is the danger that one has created a syndrome in which the "sickness" is ritualized within an artificial clinical context rather than dealt with at grass-roots level.

(c) What To Do in Cases of Overdose or "Bad Trips"

The treatment of overdose is a medical problem, but certain guide-lines should be followed by those who encounter cases of unconsciousness due to drug abuse. The patient should not be moved unless absolutely necessary but should be placed face downwards with his head turned to one side: *not* propped up in a chair or allowed to lie on his back. His collar and any tight clothing should be loosened, and an ambulance should be called. It may, in cases of mild overdose (and particularly in London) be easier to put him into a taxi and take him directly to a casualty department. The patient's breathing should be checked and his chin raised. If there is evidence nearby which helps to identify the drug used this should be taken to the hospital together with any vomited materials.[8]

Treatment of drug poisoning varies with the agent used. Amphetamine is readily absorbed from the gastro-intestinal tracts but less readily from the nasal and buccal mucosa. Urinary excretion begins within three hours of an oral dose and nearly half the dose has usually appeared within forty-eight hours. Treatment is usually by gastric lavage and phenobarbitone will probably be used. Barbiturates too are readily absorbed from the stomach and rectum but complete excretion of long-acting compounds may take a week. With phenobarbitone poisoning, prolonged coma and respiratory complications are likely. Treatment involves the giving of oxygen and restoration of blood pressure, and amphetamine may be used. With methaqualone (Mandrax) poisoning, the treatment is intensive supporting therapy without forced diuresis.[9]

In fact, to do nothing is often the most positive action in non-fatal cases. "The best treatment of non-fatal poisoning is inactivity. No drug can restore uncomplicated normal functioning faster than healthy inactivation and excretion".[10] In the treatment of drug psychosis, phenothiazones may be helpful. The B.M.A. Working Party on Amphetamines commented: "No special treatment is necessary for an amphetamine psychosis other than drug withdrawal. It may be necessary to use phenothiazines in order to control the psychosis and restlessness."[11] 50–100 mg. chlorpromezine (Largactil) or, in milder cases, 60–120 mg. of phenobarbitone will also "cut" an LSD phychosis and produce a return to relative normality. But the most valuable element in the cases of those suffering from "bad trips" is to "bring them down" gently, in a quiet room with subdued lights. By the use of low-pitched positive conversation, without quick, abrupt movements, the anxiety can be changed into assurance that they are still themselves. In areas of high incidence of psychoses a "calm centre" has been found to be of great value, and important psychological and spiritual help can be given from such a base, as the American "free clinics" have shown.

2. THE CARING COMMUNITY

> Much Christian literature on this subject lays great emphasis
> on the miraculous effect that the Christian Gospel has on
> young people. The only miracle we have witnessed is the
> painfully slow growth of self-awareness among young
> people who find it much easier to run away from their true
> selves.   SALVATION ARMY RINK CLUB[12]

The second level at which the Church in a particular
neighbourhood may be involved in helping the young drug-
taker is that of long-term care. As we have seen, there is
long-term caring too within the "problem districts" themselves. The record of the East Harlem Protestant Parish in
New York, and, on a lesser scale, of Christian groups in the
West End of London, shows the importance of creating a
caring community within the areas of crisis. But most
churches will find their role lies elsewhere, either in trying
to *prevent* some of the more serious crises from occurring,
or in the critical work of *after-care* of those who have been
addicted.

The existence of the out-patient units is not always seen
as a means to eventual abstinence from drugs. One official
report has expressed alarm that "in some quarters these
centres are being regarded as mere prescribing units without any positive objective". On the contrary, it is claimed:

> Out-patient clinics are also rehabilitation clinics . . . we visual-
> ize the out-patient clinics as being strategically placed to form
> the focal point for the whole process of rehabilitation.[13]

Clearly, if this were to be so, there would need to be
close links with families and with voluntary bodies working
within the community. The Report of the Rehabilitation
Sub-Committee concentrated very closely on hostel pro-
vision, stressing the need for short-stay hostels for homeless
addicts and for hostels in the London area for ex-addicts,[14]
but it said very little about the need for a continuing process of care of the addict within his environment. The
emphasis on "community nursing" at some of the units is,

however, an encouraging development, and represents a move in the direction of an integrated approach involving a community of disciplines. As a Ministry of Health Circular in 1967 stressed:[15] "the results in the rehabilitation of individual patients are likely to come from close collaboration from the earliest possible stage between hospital authorities, local health authorities, general practitioners, and voluntary bodies".

Three specific ways in which local Christian communities could contribute are in the fields of advice and counselling, visiting of families, and after-care. First, it is apparent that many young people desperately need an informal, non-clinical "problem centre", where many of the difficulties of adolescence can be sorted out. Here is a field where priest, psychiatrist, and trained laymen and women could very well collaborate, as has been done, for example, in the Highgate Counselling Centre.[16] More necessary than "treatment centres" are "prevention centres", particularly in the problem areas of our cities. Ideally, every church should form the focal point for such counselling work, for it is pre-eminently the cure of souls, which belongs to priest and people.

Secondly, there is a need for Christian workers who can make contact with young drug-takers and their families, and to whom their colleagues engaged in "casualty caring" can refer young people. This work requires people of tremendous patience and compassion, but endowed with commonsense and unpatronizing. The care of the families of addicts is of the utmost importance and often neglected. It is dangerous to generalize about family situations, but certain features occur with great frequency, the most obvious being the absence of a strong father-figure and the dominance of the mother.[17] The counselling of parents is an aspect of the drug scene of which little is said or written. In some cases the addict would be best helped if he were "adopted" by a stable and loving family on a more or less permanent basis.

Thirdly, the after-care of the ex-addict within the community demands a co-operative action of various groups. It is of little value to have after-care centre in the heart of the countryside unless they are in close liaison with other groups and individuals in the districts to which the young person returns. This one needs two types of group: the one located within the home community, whose role is to advise, help, and support the ex-addict; the other located away from his home, to which he may be sent, probably immediately after withdrawal, for a period of up to twelve months. Examples of the first type are the various counselling centres, youth clubs, and local churches. Within the Underground scene, Release, operating from a house in Notting Hill, runs a legal and general advice centre for young people, associated closely with a Sunday club, and a reference library providing accurate data on drugs. It is one of the fundamental objectives of Release, to develop self-awareness and responsibility with the Underground so that young people are able to help and support each other. For it scarcely needs emphasizing that no addict will be "cured" by having the values of an alien Establishment enforced upon him, but only by his acceptance of a positive and exciting way of life which removes the need for drug abuse.

It is in relationship to the building up of caring communities within each area that one sees the role of the "Rehabilitation centres". This is an appalling term and its use alienates many people. They are in essence communities in which the ex-addict can re-adjust and re-orientate his life, and be weaned back into the community. The Coke Hole centre at Ashley Copse, Andover, and Life for the World Centre at Northwick Park near Moreton-in-the-Marsh are examples of Christian communities operating on these lines, while Spelthorne St Mary, near Egham, combines an in-patient residential with an intensive after-care programme. Such programmes, however, must lean heavily for their success upon the ability of communities elsewhere to absorb the ex-addict. It is not simply the addict who must change: the community must change radically.

3. SOME PROBLEMS OF CARING

Teach us to care and not to care.
Teach us to sit still. T. S. ELIOT[18]

In conclusion, there are a number of difficulties and dangers which Christian groups within the drug scene will have to face. The first, unfortunately, is the fact that the Christian presence on the scene is not always characterized by responsibility or accuracy. In particular, a type of unintelligent evangelicalism, in which "the Gospel" is offered in a highly distorted and hysterical form, as an alternative to drug abuse, has done immense harm and left trails of casualties behind it. To offer to the addict a debased, fanatical version of Christianity is to insult his intelligence and probably to do considerable spiritual damage.

David Wilkerson's well-known book *The Cross and the Switchblade* which describes the work of a Pentecostal minister among drug-takers in New York has sometimes been read by Christians in Britain and treated as a guide book to addiction. The unintelligent use of this book by people ignorant of the scene has probably been responsible for a good deal of the harm done by some evangelical groups. It is sad, therefore, but necessary, to have to advise that not all the claims made by some of these groups will stand analysis, and the standards of factual accuracy in many cases leave a good deal to be desired. Moreover, the condescending, insensitive approach adopted by some crusaders can make the progress to union with God more difficult and can undo the work done by more mature and spiritually conscious Christian groups. A very balanced account by some young Salvationists warned that "our evangelistic ardour could be in danger of denying the individuality of the person we are confronting".[20] This criticism does not fortunately apply to all evangelical

groups, and one is hopeful that a more balanced and intelligent spirituality may be emerging.[21]

Secondly, one needs to exercise great care that, in helping the addict within the scene, one is not simply maintain-
ing, and perhaps promoting, his addiction. There are
certainly some addicts who *need* to be maintained, and
whose dependence on opiates must be accepted, for the
present at least, as a sad but necessary element in their
lives. But there is a real danger, that, with the best inten-
tions, some groups and individuals may be contributing to
the problems. The same criticism could be applied to some
of the out-patient units which are simply prescribing points
and, indirectly, centres for spreading addiction. It is, however, quite easy to say this, and very difficult at times, in
practice, to realize and avoid this danger. Christian groups
need in this connection, to ensure that their work on the
scene is characterized by a developing and increasing holiness and inner spirituality. The growth in holiness and
union with God is by far the best safeguard against any
likelihood that "identification" is misunderstood as
"acquiescence".

Thirdly, the increased attention to addiction has led to
a large number of people becoming interested in the field
for what is, often euphemistically, described as "research".
The number of "theses", "second year essays", "C.S.E. projects" and so on, which attempt to cover "drugs" in six
weeks and a thousand words can only have been exceeded
by the rash of similar studies on "immigration" in the early
1960s. In fact, the danger of "race relations" becoming a
professional subject has been repeated in regard to "drugs".
Genuine research, it need hardly be said, is vital. What is
deplorable is the number of people whose concern for
"research" seems to obliterate any real concern for the
addict as a person. The study and reporting of addiction
has become a financially profitable business, the addict
presents endless research possibilities, and any attempt to
attack this situation is at once dubbed "emotional involve-

ment". But the Christian who asserts the paramount importance of love and care for people as people needs to be in a position in which his protest cannot be dismissed as "unbalanced", "getting the situation out of proportion", and the other, all too familiar phrases.

Fourthly, the problem of "emotional involvement" needs to be understood correctly. Often "emotional involvement" is used, irrationally, as a synonym for caring. The Christian is committed to the love of his brother. It is this which defines his risen life in Christ (1 John 3.14). But his love is not the *philia* of a purely natural friendship, nor the *eros* which desires to possess the loved one, but the *agape* of complete self-giving, itself rooted in the divine self-giving. The Christian therefore loves his brother within the process of a divine love which enfolds them both. In the silence of his life hid with Christ in God (Col. 3.3) he is taught to love without the lustful frenzied desire of human possessiveness, but out of the profound contentment and calm of the Godhead. So it is that true *attachment*, true *involvement*, is only made possible by that *detachment* of the spirit, the inner purification of which St John of the Cross speaks.

This authentic detachment is quite different from the cold "professional" detachment, the debased doctrine which is so often handed out as a social work maxim, and which is rooted in a fear of the consequences of "getting involved". The true detachment of which the spiritual masters speak is a clinging to God, an absorption in the divine life, which makes a deep concern for and involvement with persons compatible with objectivity and spiritual wholeness. Without this inner *ascesis* of the spirit, the worker will crack under the heavy emotional pressure, and the drug scene is filled with such casualties.

Fifthly, it is not surprising that the drug scene, like other similar scenes, often attracts to it the emotionally unbalanced. At times, some of the "workers" seem to be more disturbed than the addicts! The caring community must care for them too. But one needs to be cautious before using every voluntary helper who offers his services: he may simply be seeking to "work through" his own problems at the expense of other people's. On the other hand, an offer of help can often be a hidden plea for help. Caution should be exercised too with regard to some of the groups and individuals operating within the scene, not all of whom are quite what they seem, and some of whom can do harm.

Finally, no amount of Christian work on the drug scene will be adequate if it does not face the Church's own need for healing. It is no use attempting to "rehabilitate" the addict by integrating him into precisely that conventional society whose values and standards he has rejected. The Church must see its ministry to the drug scene as being a purging and a learning process. Perhaps the respectable, conventional Church must die before the living Body of Christ can arise. It must certainly cease to be the community of the "good" and the "respectable" and those who conform to the dubious standards of middle-class materialism, and become, as at the beginning, the brotherhood of those who are led by the spirit and are free (Rom. 8.14; Gal. 4–5).

8

The Spirituality of the Drug Scene

1. SPIRITUAL FORCES OF THE UNDERGROUND

> More people should see us as a spiritual force for good in the world and not "dirty hippies" and "junkies".
>
> JIM GRIFFIN[1]

The title of this chapter will appear to many Christians absurd or even offensive. They see the drug-taking communities as wholly decadent, corrupt communities of lost, rebellious people. The attitude of some Christians is aptly revealed by an advertisement which appeared in 1969 for a film which would make the Gospel "relevant to teenagers drifting into a sin-stained psychedelic world of drugs and drink".[2] It is difficult to imagine a more confused and unintelligent assortment of words. Leaving aside the meaningless use of the word "psychedelic" in this context, and the quaint connection between the "psychedelic world" and "drugs *and drink*" (my italics), the assumption of these words is that the drug scene as such is "sin-stained" in a way in which the rest of society is not. The association of the words "sin", "psychedelic", "drugs", and "drink" tells its own story, and represents both an inadequate notion of sin and an almost total ignorance of the current scene.

It is significant that many hippies and other sensitive young people on the scene tend to regard the church as being very unspiritual indeed, and quite unaware of the powerful spiritual currents affecting their generation. Their acquaintance with certain types of "evangelical" approach confirm them in their belief that Christians are unintelligent, lacking spiritual perception and sensitivity, and irretrievably committed to the materialistic standards of conventional society. The Church is seen as the religious arm of the Establishment and, although many clergy and churches may be found helpful, the Church remains committed to an alien scene and can never be otherwise. The Underground, in its best moments, represents a fundamental attack on what Caroline Coon has called "a society whose moral spirit is lower and more disillusioned than it has been for a long time".[3] The Church is part of this society.

The association of drug use with a quest for self-awareness and a new religious attitude was evident in the early days of the "beat generation" in America, when "beat" was derived from "beatific" and Kerouac's simple, crazy figures had an almost messianic character.[4] The hipster, an anarchist writer commented in 1960,[5] was seeking the salvation of his soul. In this quest for a new sense of spiritual identity, cannabis was of particular importance. In using "pot" as a spiritual aid the beats were not original. A whole tradition in the East lay behind them. In Britain, the infamous Aleister Crowley (1875–1947), who had delved into occultism, Buddhism, and pharmacology, had written a study on the psychology of cannabis which he saw as valuable only as "a preliminary demonstration that there exists another world attainable—somehow".[6]

Eastern ideas have played a central role in shaping an Underground spiritual attitude. Zen Buddhism appealed to the beats, generally mediated by such writers as Suzuki and Alan Watts. Zen has continued to figure in the Underground scene, but 1968 and 1969 has seen a revival of the "Krishna Consciousness" movement, and the chanting of "Hare Krishna" has made moderate numbers of disciples in the London area. Zen represents the awareness of pure being beyond subject and object. The disciple's concern is with *satori* (enlightenment), not as a means of self-illumination—though a good deal of the Underground's superficial quasi-Zen has remained self-absorbed—but as the removal of all objects through contemplation of the void, and the transcendence of personal consciousness altogether. In association with the use of cannabis and LSD, the search for "nothingness" beyond the confines of the ego fitted into the emerging Underground scene very happily. Hence the interest among so many on the scene in meditation, fasting, and other spiritual disciplines. Indeed, "pot" itself is part of the ritual, part of the religious culture which has grown up around this new quest for self-awareness and identity. But it is a religion which is fundamentally atheistic, which is why Buddha can claim, if anyone can, to be the architect of the Underground.

But the Eastern influence goes deeper than this. It is related to the search for *unity*, for a "meta-egoic" experience in which the self loses itself into union with all existence. This is what the LSD experience is about: one writer has pointed out that "the LSD mystical experience leans towards pantheism unless there are religious images already established".[7] Hence the appeal of Hindu ideas, in which "god", Brahman, appears as existence, the Godhead within all creation. In the Bhaghavad-Gita, the disciple is taught to attain a super-conscious state, *samadhu*, which is union with the Godhead. The Underground abounds with this concern for transcendence of the ego.

The mystically-oriented scene feels a close affinity with the East, as the migration of hippies to Afghanistan, Pakistan, and India in search of gurus indicates. "The people of the East are our friends", one Underground writer pointed out.[8] "We are more like them than we are like the average Westerner and, because they are much closer to the truth, they can be turned on much easier and also there is *so* much we can learn from them. We, who are out there, should communicate with *all* people good and bad and so strengthen the bond between us and the East. . . . Living with the people and with genuine love radiating from heart to heart is the only way." The Eastern influence is most clearly shown in the musical developments of the Underground scene. Thus, "The Quintessence", interviewed recently, said[9]

> We are all into a mantra thing. We all have our own mantras which we use for everyday. On Sundays we have a big get-together with all our friends chanting mantras, some of them similar to those of the Krishna chanters. Then we usually meditate some and generally have a good time. The mantras and the Indian influence play very important parts in our music.

Other groups have not been reluctant to express their conception of spiritual reality. Thus Marc Bolan of Tyrannosaurus Rex, a group which has been considerably influenced by Tolkien's Lord of the Rings:

> I do believe in the Guardian Angel scene. . . . Christ must have been a gas. I think he was a very turned-on guy, and very much with God. God is the coolest thing of all. I think if I'm just a splinter out of his head, then he must be a bit like me, not much though. I see him as a monster sun that opens in the middle and you could get sucked into it and out the other side. Where you come out, I don't know, that's only my imagery. But it's a preparation for birth. We're only people and that's a bit of a drag. . . . You are born and born again until you reach the ultimate, until you reach another scene, get into another dimension.[10]

This search for new scenes, new experiences, new dimensions, is at the heart of the Underground's spiritual movement.

One expression of this search appears in the "Mystical scene Magazine" Gandalf's Garden. This magazine is not typical of the Underground as a whole, but it represents and articulates one important tradition and tendency within it. Its inspiration is, of course, Gandalf the white wizard from Lord of the Rings, "the mythological hero of the age". Its editorial policy is clear:

In the land of Middle Earth under threat of engulfment by the dark powers, Gandalf unites the differing races, mistrustful of each other through lack of understanding and communication, in a final effort to save the world. The crusader spirit in Gandalf is echoed in the cry of the New Generation seeking an Alternative to the destructive forces of to-day's world, by spreading human love and aid for the unity of all the peoples of the Earth.[11]

Gandalf's Garden represents "the magical garden of our inner worlds, overgrowing into the world of manifestation ... soulflow from the pens of creators—mystics, writers, artists, diggers, delvers, and poets". This group are concerned with inner revolution and complain of the "Mordorminds of the soul-sick".[12] They see the unrest in the world as the result of emotional vibrations and thoughts from the etheric field, and they see the role of "the evolving Brotherhood of the Spirit" to be the propagation of a spiritual revolution which will see its crowning glory in the New Age soon to come. A poster announcing "Gandalf's Garden Grows Here", displayed in a window, identifies the inhabitant as a "fellow-conspirator of love".[13] The pages of this magazine contain frequent references to reincarnation, the Age of Aquarius, Buddhism, meditation, and the Arthurian legend.

Associated with this spiritual ferment, the Underground has been penetrated by efforts to build an "Alternative Society". The Anti-University marked stages on the way, and the setting up of "Release", BIT (a twenty-four-hour information Service). Middle Earth, and the Arts Labs have certainly represented a developing social consciousness. The Diggers, a group which was formed out of this need to strengthen social aims, held a forum in April, 1968, explaining:

It was a sad winter which saw the hopes of the Love Revolution blighted. Expansion of awareness within the Psychedelic Movement had got strung out on chemicals, unable to soar to the heights of total spiritual freedom; and the promise of

Flower Power had wilted like the last rose of summer. Drop-outs from the System had nowhere to drop into and the socio-economic pressures of the System screwed up many an isolated small group or lone individual trying to do beautiful things. The time was at hand for all love revolutionaries to pool their resources and work closely together to build more free communes within the Alternative Society for their dharma brothers and sisters. The first step obviously was to bring beautiful people into contact with each other. And what better way to do this than to bring them face to face under one roof at a forum on communal living.[14]

It is likely that as the Underground becomes more purposeful and mature its ability to build structures of renewal will increase, and it could become one of the most powerful forces of change. There are signs that whole sections of the scene are becoming less "strung out on chemicals" and that the search for a new pattern of life is only at its beginning. It is a sad fact that, with a few notable exceptions, the institutional Church has remained insulated from these powerful spiritual movements and is probably unaware of their existence.

2. THE PSYCHEDELIC EXPERIENCE AND THE MYSTICAL STATE

A psychedelic experience is a journey to new realms of consciousness. . . . Such experiences of enlarged consciousness can occur in a variety of ways: sensory deprivation, yoga, exercises, disciplined meditation, religious or aesthetic ecstasies, or spontaneously. Most recently they have become available to anyone through the ingestion of psychedelic drugs such as LSD, psilocybin, mescaline, DMT etc.

LEARY, METZNER, AND ALPERT, *The Psychedelic Experience*[15]

Do you really think that the "gates of perception" open cold to a nit like you as a consequence of sucking a Tate & Lyle cube impregnated with a Swiss chemical?

COLIN MACINNES[16]

One of the most complex questions about the use of psyche-delic drugs concerns the relationship of the experience to those states of consciousness recounted by the spiritual masters of East and West. In principle, the problems con-fronted William James in the *Varieties of Religious Experi-ence* published in 1902 and, in some ways, the debate has not progressed very far since James. Indeed, it has been pointed out that "all the issues raised by psychedelic experience are raised in a pamphlet quoted by James, *The Anaesthetic Revelation and the Gist of Philosophy* by Benjamin Paul Blood published in 1874".[17] The theory is that there are potential forms of consciousness which need stimulus, regions of the mind which know mysticism and madness. Mind-expanding drugs are seen as agents which might remove the screens obscuring higher regions of con-sciousness. They are "agents which reveal but do not chart the mental regions".[18] For James and Blood the agent under discussion was nitrous oxide. It was Aldous Huxley in *The Doors of Perception* and *Heaven and Hell* who reopened the question of the "genuineness" of drug-induced mystic-ism. Yet it is probably true to say that "in understanding the essence of the experience we have learnt little since William James".[19]

Of his own experience with nitrous oxide James wrote:

Looking back on my own experiences they all converge towards a kind of insight to which I cannot help ascribing some meta-physical significance. The keynote of it is invariably a reconciliation. It is as if the opposites of the world, whose contradictoriness and conflict make all our difficulties and troubles, were melted into unity.[20]

This description is very similar to many used by contem-porary LSD-takers. It is important to emphasize the "meta-physical significance" which many young "acid-heads" would ascribe to their use of psychedelics. Allan Cohen has stressed the mistake of seeing psychedelic drug use in terms of "escape" and has suggested that it should be seen instead

8

as the beginning of a quest for expansion of consciousness.[21] Certainly the claims made by advocates of psychedelic drug use are fundamentally spiritual ones. One writer has claimed that LSD helps one to discover the central human experience which the Zen masters call *satori* and Hindus call *moksha*, and which alters all other experiences.[22] The well-known writer, Alan Watts, has called the experience "cosmic consciousness":

> There is really no satisfactory name for this type of experience. To call it mystical is to confuse it with the visions of another world, or of God and angels. To call it spiritual or metaphysical is to suggest that it is not also extremely concrete, while the term "cosmic consciousness" itself has the unpoetic flavour of occultist jargon.[23]

There is no essential difference, Watts argues, between experiences *under favourable conditions* through chemicals, and those experiences described by William James, Evelyn Underhill, and the exponents of mysticism, and he suggests that psychedelic trips might most profitably take place in a retreat house with the guidance of a religiously orientated psychiatrist.[24]

The religious nature of the psychedelic experience is most clearly expressed in the writings and claims of Timothy Leary, the former Harvard psychologist, who is regarded throughout the scene as the prophet of the psychedelic revolution. Leary categorically states that the ecstatic process which for centuries has been produced by such techniques as fasting, contemplative focussing of attention, yoga exercises, and so on, techniques which alter body chemistry, can now be brought about by drug ingestion, and this "drug-induced *ecstasis* is now called the *psychedelic experience*". He sees it as primarily a religious experience, defining the term thus:[26]

> The religious experience is the ecstatic, incontrovertibly certain, subjective discovery of answers to four basic spiritual questions,

questions, that is, about ultimate power, life, human destiny, and the ego. He suggests that between 40 and 90 per cent of psychedelic subjects report intense religious experiences and it is this belief that led to the foundation of the League for Spiritual Discovery.

In the League for Spiritual Discovery, ashrams are set up in which renunciants, that is "drop-outs", must abandon secular activities and live a communal life. The cult is described as "an orthodox psychedelic religion" and its "sacraments . . . are psychedelic chemicals which at every turning point in human history have been provided by God for man's illumination and liberation". The rituals of the cult are twofold. First, the disciple attains sensory illumination, goes "out of his mind" in order "to come to his senses" for a period of at least one hour each day, with such aids as cannabis, DMT, meditation, prayer, incense, and so on. Secondly, one day a week he spends in solitude using LSD, peyote, and psilocybin. Thus in the League, the psychedelic experience has become the focal point of an intense spiritual quest.[27] Leary would not claim that all users of LSD, however, attain such heights. Indeed, on one occasion, he talked of "high church" and "low church" LSD scenes!

> Ken Kesey's acid-test-rock-and-roll-freak-out is low church psychedelic, gutty, shouting, sawdust, hail, roll-on-the-floor ecstasy. Alan Watts is highest Anglican-precise, ceremonial, serene, aesthetic, classic, aristocratic with a wink.[28]

If the psychedelic claim is valid then "the chemical religious experience is a possibility".[29] All experiences involve the biochemistry of the mind. Why should not a Westerner in one hour achieve states of transcendence which would take an Easterner years of ascetic labour? Leary and his colleagues offer the use of chemicals as an alternative way of illumination. Great emphasis is laid on "set" and "setting", internal and external conditions. Quiet reading, relaxation, music, meditation or bathing, and audo-visual aids such as the *mantra* and *mandala* (a *mantra* in which sound vibrations are used in a manner akin to prayer, a *mandala* when a visual map is used for contemplation) are all recommended as preparation. But it is the precise nature of the experience which is crucial. Is it akin to a religious experience? Can it even be said to *be* a religious experience?

In the states of transcendence described by the spiritual masters a number of features are found to be present. There is a sense of *oneness* with God or the universe, combined with a *transcendence* of time and space. There is *insight*, a sense of *mystery*, and *ineffability*. There is a profound *joy*, peace, and sense of rejoicing and there is a *lasting effect* on thinking and attitude, although the experience itself is transient.[30] Pahnke's research at Harvard has certainly shown that many LSD experiences do contain some or all of these features, and this has been claimed by other writers. Masters and Houston[31] would even claim that "the process leading towards mystical culmination is far richer in the case of the psychedelic subject that is the *via negativa* or path of obliteration of the traditional mystic", while the Christian psychiatrist, Frank Lake, has described his own LSD experience thus.[32]

> On the more cheerful side, LSD abreaction also frequently permitted a regression into a beatific state of monistic identification with unlimited life as it existed in the womb and sometimes in the early months after it. It is this effect which has gained for LSD the appellation of "instant Zen". It was into this glorious liberating experience that I myself was plunged when I took the drug in the presence of a psychiatric colleague. It seemed rather unfair to be enjoying what I gather to be the goal of nature mysticism and probably also of the Hindu *advaita* without undergoing the rigours of sensory deprivation or of fasting. "God" in the ground of my being was sheer bliss. It was a faceless bliss, but who wants a face at this stage? This is the life by identification with the source of life itself without boundaries to the ego, without limitation or frustration.

Lake, however, is making a distinctly modest claim for the religious content of the LSD experience, for he relates it to nature or monistic mysticism. It is in fact at this point that the attack on drug-induced mysticism was made by Professor R. C. Zaehner. Zaehner was disturbed by Huxley's claim that the effect of mescaline was closely comparable to a genuine mystical experience. "If he is right," he warned, "the conclusions ... are alarming".[33] But Zaehner was reassured by his own trivial experience on mescaline and by his conviction that drugs could only induce the *lower* types of mystical state, nature mysticism and monistic mysticism, and not the *theistic* type. Zaehner's rejection of the chemical claims has been criticized as special pleading. In particular, it has been shown that numerous experiences with psychedelic drugs do show all the features of theistic and Christian mystical states.

The most violent attack on the chemical approach to spirituality has, however, come from within the psychedelic scene itself. In 1965 a young enthusiast went to Nepal in search of the mystical way with the aid of cannabis and LSD, and he visited the Indian mystic Meher Baba. The journey has been described, somewhat extravagantly, as "a pilgrimage which became a focal point for the downfall of the psychedelic fantasy".[34] It certainly became a focal point for the initiation of a campaign against psychedelic mysticism by Meher Baba, supported in the United States by one of his disciples, Allan Cohen, a young psychologist involved in counselling the hippy community in Berkeley. Meher Baba, who died in 1968, lived at Ahmednagar and had maintained a total silence from 1925. He has been described as "the best non-acid authority available to compare the results of chemical stimulation of the deeper layers of being with those produced by techniques known and used throughout time by spiritual leaders".[35] The basis of Baba's attack on the acid scene is contained in a small pamphlet *God in a Pill?* which has been circulated widely in San Francisco and at Berkeley.

Baba saw drugs as a harmful attempt to create a short-cut to spiritual reality which can only bring about a semblance of reality and hinder true development. His condemnation is a total one.

> All so-called spiritual experiences generated by taking mind-changing drugs such as LSD, mescaline, and psilocybin are superficial and add enormously to one's addiction to the deceptions of illusion which is but a shadow of reality.... The experience is as far removed from reality as a mirage from water. No matter how much one pursues the mirage one will never reach water and the search for God through drugs must end in disillusionment.[35]

Sometimes the psychedelic experiences represent "experiences of the shadows of the subtle (emotion, energy) plane in the gross (physical) world. These experiences have nothing at all to do with spiritual advancement".[37] Baba explains:

> The experiences derived through the drugs are experiences by one in the gross world of the shadows of the subtle planes and are not continuous. The experiences of the subtle sphere by one on the subtle planes are continuous, but even these experiences are of illusion, for Reality is beyond them. And so, though LSD may lead one to feel a better man personally, the feeling of having had a glimpse of reality may not only lull one into a false security but also will, in the end, derange one's mind. Although LSD is not an addiction-forming drug, one can become attached to the *experiences* arising from its use and one gets tempted to use it in increasing doses, again and again, in the hope of deeper and deeper experiences. But eventually this causes madness or death.[38]

Drug use, on this view, represents the perversion of consciousness, for it stimulates centres in the brain which are usually only activated as a by-product of spiritual development where safeguards are developed.

Cohen, who used LSD in the early days of Leary's work at Harvard, now complains of "psychedelic hypocrisy".

"Too many times have I seen psychedelic mysticism generate hypocrisy in action."[39] What, he asks, is the effect of LSD on ordinary life? What is the perspective of "enlightened" souls? On the basis of his observations he concludes that the LSD path denies internal worth, leads to separateness and exclusiveness, to passivity and slavery to chemicals. The experience, moreover, is temporary and irrelevant to real living; psychedelic chemicals, he argues, "simply don't work". On the other hand, his research at Haight-Ashbury showed some interesting facts. Of forty LSD users of average age 18, 80 per cent believed in God and 92 per cent in mysticism. 82 per cent thought that mystics accepted the LSD experience and over 70 per cent said that they would stop using the drug if a known mystic said that it was spiritually harmful. Cohen has claimed that "the vanguard of the serious hippie movement (whom we might call 'meta-hippies') with a few notable exceptions are rejecting its use".[40]

How should we view the psychedelic claims from the standpoint of a Christian spirituality? One needs to distinguish two issues. The first is the nature of the experience as such and its relationship to religious experience. The second is the context of both experiences, the role of the psychedelic experience within the "acid" scene, and of religious experience within the context of developing religious life. On the first issue, it does not appear to me to be an adequate answer to the psychedelic claims to say that the experience which they describe is wholly different from that described by the mystics. What is occurring in the LSD experience, as has been shown, is the process of ego-loss, of the dissolution of the conscious self in a kind of death experience. Leary uses *The Tibetan Book of the Dead* as a guide to spiritual death and rebirth. It is here that one enters the borderland between mysticism and psychosis. What are called "bad trips" are, in fact, the crises encountered by those who have lost their ego without regaining it. So a famous *Times* leader "Blessings in shades of Green"[41] suggested that the parallel is not in fact with Christian or Eastern mysticism, or with the natural mysticism of Wordsworth, but with the mysticism of the psychoses. But this is not wholly adequate, since it ignores the use of the psychedelic drugs under controlled conditions, with adequate spiritual preparation and guidance.

It is the second issue, the context of the experience, which is crucial, and here three points ought to be made. First, the role played by "experiences" in the Christian spiritual traditions of both East and West is a minor one. *The Cloud of Unknowing* refers to types of "counterfeit contemplation", "sham spirituality" in which the mind is strained, deceived by "false lights and sounds" and "materialistic distortions". The author uses language which suggests the "psychotic mysticism" with which we are familiar: ". . . it is an unnatural thing, and the devil is its chief agent. It is the quickest way to die, physically and spiritually, and drives a man mad."[42] Again, St John of the Cross warns against dependence on "apprehensions", *even when given supernaturally to the senses,* and claims that such dependence creates "a complete impediment to the attainment of spirituality".[43] The emphasis in fact throughout the spiritual writers is against exaggerating the *experience* as such. Rather it is seen in the framework of a spiritual life rooted in the discipline of prayer and sacrament. Experiences, visions, ecstasies, hallucinations, and so on are seen as common in the spiritual life. They must not be sought after nor condemned, and *dependence* on them impedes spiritual advancement. This advice would seem to apply to drug-induced experiences as much as any other.

Moreover, the writers even stress that the ascetic disciplines such as fasting and meditation, are only preliminaries to the life of prayer. Thus Archbishop Anthony Bloom writes of fasting:

The thirst ascesis is a necessary condition to progress in inner prayer. . . . To pray without fasting and keeping vigil is impossible, but even more impossible is it to fast and keep vigil unless one be permeated by the spirit of prayers.[44]

But he emphasizes:

Is it necessary to repeat that all these techniques do *not* constitute life in God any more than they constitute prayer or meditation? They are part of a rich liberative ascesis which embraces the whole being and which is by nature negative. Once attention is unified at the locus of perfect concentration and ready to receive grace and raise its prayer, then spiritual work but *begins*.[45]

This places the use of any means, chemical or non-chemical, to the attainment of spirituality in its proper context. It is only when these disciplines have aided the growth of union with God that the soul begins to be raised to pure prayer. Disciplines which do not aid this growth must be abandoned.

Secondly, there is no theological reason, in principle, why certain chemicals, under properly controlled conditions, might not play some role in spiritual development, provided the nature of the role is appreciated. It would be analogous to the use of other ascetical techniques which modify body chemistry. So far very few Christians have paid attention to the spiritual implications of psychedelics.[46] One of the most balanced and rarely noted statements of a Christian position came from an *episcopus vagans*, Michael Francis Itkin of the Evangelical Catholic Communion in Philadelphia, in evidence given to a sub-committee on LSD in 1966. Itkin, who claimed that some of his clergy had used psychedelic drugs linked with deep meditation and the sacraments, quoted Numbers 9.8–11 ("bitter herbs") as "the clearest testimony of the Bible to the psychedelic experience for the Christian". (This is nonsense!) He went on to compare the state of ego-dissolution with the teaching on the dark night of the senses and of the soul.

The mystical experience is always a case of God's grace and light breaking through the narrow barriers of our personal ego, and, to paraphrase Dietrich Bonhoeffer, there is no such thing as *cheap grace*. Howbeit, the psychedelic experience can be a temporary breaking down of the numerous blocks against transcendent reality which the personal ego of man has erected, particularly in our Western world. With the breaking down, the grace and light of God can have a free chance to operate in the consciousness of man. The psyche-delic experiences are in themselves neither good nor bad, safe nor dangerous; it depends solely on how they are used.[47]

Here psychedelics are placed within the context of a disciplined ascetical process. The danger, however, lies in the fact that the psychedelic cult shows all the signs of falling into precisely the error against which all spiritual writers warn: that of treating the experience as an end in itself and becoming dependent upon it, "strung out on chemicals",[48] and so incapable of real spiritual growth. Just as the Dionysian cult used alcohol, so the psychedelic cult uses LSD. Religious *experience* becomes more important than religious *life* and, as Cohen rightly emphasizes, there is no evidence at all to suggest that the LSD experience as such does, in itself, improve, illuminate, sanctify, or even encourage such trends. "By their fruits . . . "—indeed.

Thirdly, the spiritual reality behind the psychedelic experience is independent of the drugs used to reveal it. It resides in the state of "ego loss" and what R. D. Laing[49] calls the "meta-egoic" (beyond the ego) experience. Laing has pointed out that the critical spiritual need of the present is for maps of the meta-egoic world, maps which will enable real progress to be made. Most explorers in the psychedelic world do not go to the Christian texts but to the *Tibetan Book of the Dead*, the *I Ching*, the *Tao Te Ching*, the *Secret of the Golden Flower*, and so on. But he suggests that the death and rebirth syndrome which is the heart of the experience is something about which the Christian tradition ought to have a good deal to say. What is Baptism but death and rebirth? What is the Eucharist but the sacrifice of the ego—"our souls and bodies"—in union with the dying and rising of Christ? The psychedelic experience is that into which all Christians have been plunged and in which all can share. Surely the most critical need is for the resurrection of a Christian spiritual tradition which would give depth, discipline, and direction to the "meta-hippy" quest, the "journey beyond trips".

3. DESTRUCTION AND DEATH: THE HEROIN EXPERIENCE

> I have made a decision.
> I am going to try to nullify my life.
>
> *The Velvet Underground*, "Heroin"[50]

With heroin addiction there is a reduction of symbols to a small range. Burroughs points out that "there are less and less images as someone gets more heavily addicted".[51] The central themes which emerge so clearly in addict poetry are of loneliness, isolation, hopelessness, and self-destruction. There is confusion and torment, as in this section of a poem from hospital:

> While I was laying amongst green blankets
>   which stretched for thousands of
> years and I never felt warm—so cold—
>
> I listened to the neurotic past
>   and scratched my temple with a
> rusty darning needle and I thought
>
> and thought about all the sad
> things, entities, in wonderment; all the
> self-destruction and self-piteous wailings.
>
> I looked in a mirror and it was smashed in a
> million places and I saw a mask with all
>   the lights within distorted,
>
> all the planes and angles
>   converging and arguing
> with each other. . . .

> aah—all the blue blood and transparent veins
> shouting to be released; all the tears
> pulling at their own personal prison.

Bert Jansch in his well-known song "Needle of Death" talks of the freeing of the soul through death: "man's desire to free his mind, to release his very soul" leads him ultimately to the needle as the only liberator of conflict.

The spiritual path of the junkie is one with no vision, for there is nothing beyond. One former addict, not long off heroin, wrote of the terrifying loneliness without the drug.

> Loneliness,
> I feel it and cry it.
> I want people,
> Someone to love and care for.
> I miss my life,
> My Junk scene
> And I want to score so bad,
> Score anything.
> I need help and yet I cannot get it
> For I am shy to go to people.
> And Life is Junk
> And Junk is death.
> I walk through the city
> I know people yet know no one.

The same person wrote of two Christian friends who loved her but, in spite of their love, there remained a basic need for heroin.

> But beyond them I see no heaven
> Just a long black empty hell.
> No light—for there is no cocaine
> And coke provides the flash.
> There can be no peace
> For there is no heroin.
> There is nothing there.

Here heroin symbolizes peace, cocaine light. Life without them is devoid of purpose.

The heroin scene is one of utter hopelessness, death without rebirth, a descent into hell. One girl, now off heroin, wrote this meditation on Good Friday:

> As the clouds gathered together and prayed, drawing together their dark thundering brows to meditate upon the sweeping sickness of a generation and of thousands of bent wailing walkingsticks—aids for the physical and moulting: to the psychology books and green and honeydoped brown bottles all drifting away on an endless sea . . . a wavering tide. . . . On the words which hang in the air between the two of us: a dream that started somewhere under the black dripping longing listing pillars of mist, rotting away as everyone else has done to the strains of a whining careless love needle of Death. . . . The disciples lament from one death to a new Birth—and they've all gone now. . . .

She went on to describe:

> . . . the MAN weaned on wine, justified by junk, happy on hash, hung-up on heroin, crucified by cocaine, and morbidly, on the telephone, to the mortuary with a final shot of morphine, to a gaunt ghastly grave from the rising soil.

These poems speak only of death and of the aloneness which is hell. They represent the spirituality of dying, the world of those who have not risen again, who live in the darkness and there is no light.

9

The Priest
and the Drug Scene

The sole end of priesthood is the contemplation of the
Divine.
                                                MARIE DE LA TRINITE

Finally, we need to ask: What is the precise contribution of
the priest to the drug scene? The accusation is frequently
made that the priest whose ministry involves caring about
drug abuse, or racialism, or bad housing, is indulging in
"social work", and is simply "a social worker in a dog-
collar". Two immediate points must be made about this
accusation. First, it is an odd mentality which sees activities
such as these as "social work", but looks upon the multi-
tude of unpriestly activities such as running fêtes and
bazaars, organizing parties, youth clubs, Bingo, and the
like, as in some sense *not* "social work". In fact, the priest
on the drug scene probably spends less time on useless kinds
of social work than the average priest does. Secondly, there
is an artificial distinction made here between the priest's
role and the social worker's role. In practice there is considerable overlap, since the priest is concerned with the
whole person, with man in society orientated Godwards.
He is concerned with the reconciliation of all things in
Christ. Too often the nature of the pastoral role is seen
through the eyes of false spirituality, the priest being concerned with the "spiritual", the social worker with the
"material" side of man's existence. Clearly, this is unsound
theology and in practice worthless. But what is the nature

of priesthood? We need to look at three primary aspects of his role: as *pastor*, as *spiritual guide*, and as mediator of the *sacraments*.

1. PRIESTHOOD AND PASTORAL CARE

The mishandling of spiritual transitional states has other results than the arrest of spiritual growth and maturation. The alien mental contents which are being ejected in the course of sanctification are, in the minds of untrained clergymen, labelled "for psychiatrists only". The whole significance of what is going on in this Christian person is missed. The Holy Spirit is moving in and the clergyman is frantically engaged in trying to stop the dispossessed "devils" from being pushed out.   DR FRANK LAKE[1]

The Christian priest shares in the sacrificial work of Christ in his Body: his priesthood merely focusses the priesthood of the whole Body of Christ. What is priesthood? "It is the office which ritually, inwardly, and ascetically shares the dying and rising of Christ."[2] The priest acts at the sacrificial centre, within the pattern of death and rebirth, and his most fundamental work is secret, hidden with Christ in God (Col. 3.3). It is impossible to explain the nature and function of priesthood to someone who does not understand the nature of sacrifice, of death and rebirth, the cycle of redemption. Apart from this, the priest is meaningless, he stands for nothing. It is the loss of spiritual perception which has led many young priests to lose grip on their role. For the practice of priesthood is inseparable from the theology of sacrifice.

The priest thus has a specific role to play, for he mediates the world of the Spirit within this world, he stands at the point of intersection of the old and new creations. But his role will inevitably overlap a good deal with those of psychiatrist, psychotherapist, social worker, probation officer, and so on. It is important, though at times difficult, to see the distinction in roles and not to confuse them. It is certainly true, for example, that "the clergy cannot do their work at all without doing some form of psychotherapy".[3] Similarly, a good deal of the priest's work will be "social". This is all the more reason for careful study and clarification of the point of his own ministry.

Considerable harm has been done, not only among young people, but over a wide field, by a deplorable caricature of the priestly image. Priests are seen as cold, aloof, unbending, almost sub-human, and some priests seem to regard the cultivation of sub-human characteristics as a part of their sacerdotal character. In fact, priesthood implies utter humanity, for the source of priesthood is the Incarnate Christ, who learnt obedience through human suffering (Heb. 5.8), and who raised humanity into the Godhead. To be a priest should make one more, not less, human. As Teilhard de Chardin put it:[4]

> To the full extent of my power *because I am a priest*, I wish from now on to be the first to become conscious of all that the world loves, pursues, and suffers: I want to be the first to seek, to sympathize and to suffer; the first to open myself out and sacrifice myself—to become more widely human and more nobly of the earth then the world's servants.

So often, however, "becoming a clergyman" sets the seal on the creeping suffocation of real life. The real man begins to die and the clerical caricature takes over.

In the approach to young people on the drug scene the priest needs to develop certain qualities, and they are qualities which apply generally, not merely in this ministry. First, he must be completely *natural*. (Grace perfects nature, and does not destroy it.) There is nothing more pathetic than the superficial assumed "with-it-ness" of some young clergy whose stance breathes insincerity and unreality, and young people are the first to see through facades of this kind. This is not to say that more hippy priests, more beat priests, more gay priests, more revolutionary priests are not desperately needed, but they must come naturally from within the scene. The priest must never pretend to be what he is not, for the sake of popularity, impact, or "relevance". The old-fashioned "straight", "square" priest has a very important role to play on the scene.

Secondly, he must be *non-condescending*. The young people whom he meets are not there to be "done good to", or to be patronized. Much Christian work has had a patronizing, pity-the-poor-junkie, soup-kitchen mentality. The young people on the scene must be viewed as human beings, and loved for their own sakes. The priest, if he is humble, will learn as much from them as they will from him. But humility and willingness to learn are crucial. In any case, young people in cafés and clubs will not take at all kindly to the condescending approach of a clergyman, and if he behaves in this way they will tell him exactly where to go.

Thirdly, he must at all costs avoid the "parsonical" approach and manner, and if he has adopted it, he should rid himself of it. The conventional image of the priest, in his sober black suit, keeping "respectable" hours and generally being the epitome of social goodness, will be quite valueless and even harmful on the drug scene. The parsonical voice and outlook is, in any case, a music-hall joke. But the priest needs to shed much that is akin to it: the preoccupation with a "schedule", the tendency to "talk at" people and never to have real human communication, the cultivation of the ecclesiastical expression. Perhaps one useful way in which this could be partially achieved would be by the avoidance of many of the ecclesiastical gatherings. They encourage the growth of a "clerical club", their insulated atmosphere helps to sever the priest even further from the real world, and the influence of some of them is poisonous. As the late Canon Stanley Evans once complained of some clergyman, "only surrounded by clergymen can he be happy: the superficial *bonhomie* of the common-room or the gossip of the sacristy appears to be necessary to his salvation".[5]

Fourthly, he needs a ridiculously well-developed *sense of humour*. In the Soho clubs "micky-taking" is often the be-

9

ginning of pastoral contact and can be of enormous value also in breaking down barriers. Young people will often deliberately tell dirty jokes—occasionally quite good ones! —to a priest in order to "try him out". If the priest is shocked or embarrassed or responds with a weak smile, they know what to expect. If he is found to be reasonably unshocked and to have a good sense of humour, it will be greatly to his advantage. A sense of humour is also important for two other reasons. Work on the drug scene puts a priest under very heavy pressure, and he is liable to break down at certain points. A "goonish" ability to laugh at the absurd and not to take himself too seriously is tremendously helpful and will keep him sane! It will also be good for the priest's humility if he is "cut down to size" frequently by young people who do not pay him the conventional "respect" to which he may have been accustomed.

Finally, above all he must be seen as *utterly trustworthy* and reliable. The priest who is available at a particular crisis and knows exactly what to do has immediately acquired a reputation among many young people whom he probably does not know. The building up of trust and confidence is a slow, painful process, and requires tremendous patience and compassion. The priest must be ready always to see the action of the Spirit in the crises of the scene. At root, so many of the agonies and frustrations have deeply spiritual roots, and here the priest who is quiet and compassionate may find developing a new style of pastoral care, caring for the souls of people who would never come near a church, but whose hearts God is drawing, and whose anguish Christ shares.

2. PRIESTHOOD AND SPIRITUALITY

How many priests have first-hand awareness of such meta-egoic experiences which thousands of young people seem desperately to need, and go to extreme lengths to get even to risking terms of imprisonment if they take the drug route? ... How many people ever go to priests for guidance in these respects, for orientation? How many priests know about this even at second or third hand?   DR R. D. LAING[6]

It has been suggested in the previous pages that a good deal of the contemporary scene is concerned with the search for spiritual experiences. If this is true there would appear *prima facie* to be an important role for some clergy to play in helping to guide and direct young people on the spiritual way. Evidence from other directions suggests that there is a revival of interest in prayer and contemplation. What are the consequences of all this for the spiritual tradition and for priests?

First, it is obvious that any priest who is to be valuable on the scene must absorb and learn from its life and culture. He must learn from the spiritual ideas which are going around: he ought, for instance, to study something about Zen, about the Eastern approaches to the higher consciousness and, on a different level, about the important moral and social ideals which figure in contemporary folk-pop culture. From the quest for drug-induced experience, he might learn more of the authentic Christian mystical tradition.

For, secondly, the present scene calls for a revival of deep spirituality and of contemplative prayer. The religious orders might consider whether they may have a crucial role to play in the spiritual enlightenment of those sections of the Underground which feel the need of direction beyond drug-induced spiritual experience. Already the Dominicans in Oxford are playing a key part in the Oxford hippy scene. The priest is in a strategically important position to help in the understanding of the complex issues of life and death, of dying and rebirth, of darkness and emptiness which figure prominently in the drug scene. He will be able to refer the searcher to the masters of the spiritual life. For it is clear that much in the psychedelic quest represents a striving after the mystical path in which "God will lead the soul by a most lofty path of dark contemplation and aridity, wherein it seems to be lost".[7] The description of the religious experiences under LSD at once suggests the need for progress towards the interior life, progress which is described most clearly in Carmelite spirituality. Thus St John of the Cross writes of the dark night through which the soul is led:

> These three parts of the night are all one night; but like night itself, it has three parts. For the first part, which is that of sense, is comparable to the beginning of night, the point at which things begin to fade from sight. And the second part, which is faith, is comparable to midnight, which is total darkness. And the third part is like the close of night, which is God, the which part is now near to the light of day.[8]

But the psychedelic experience, whether aided by drugs or not, can only reveal the spiritual regions. It cannot chart the path of illumination, and it is at this point that guidance in the interior life is needed. Indeed, the scene now calls for a new kind of spiritual direction in which the insights of Christian spiritual theology can be applied to the post-LSD situation.

The priest cannot be a spiritual guide unless his own life is steeped in prayer and contemplation. The whole shape of his office is determined by the inner spirituality of his life. Ulrich Simon in his *A Theology of Auschwitz* refers to the importance of the priest's office in the appalling horror of the concentration camp:[9]

> The priestly ideal uses and converts the nothingness which the world of Auschwitz offers. Here the priest's sacerdotal dedication encounters the vacuum with self-sacrifice. . . . The priest at the camp counts because he has no desires of self-importance and gives life because he stands already beyond extermination. He is the exact opposite to the king-rat. The hour of darkness cannot take him by surprise since he has practised silence in darkness.

In his work on the drug scene, the priest is to be a symbol of light beyond the darkness, because he mediates the light of Christ risen, and so "he stands already beyond extermination". The strengthening of his own inner spiritual resources cannot be over-stressed, for what he is counts for far more than what he does. Like the entire Christian community, he is engaged in a warfare of the Spirit, and his weapons are those of prayer, fasting, and sacrifice.

Intercessory prayer within the drug scene is of incalculable importance. The priest as the focal point of a disciplined, interceding group can spread his net over a very wide area. Often the most powerful act that one person can do for another is to intercede, for in so doing he operates at a level below and beyond human actions.

> The intercessor spreads out over an ever-widening field the enfolding web of the love of God, and receives in his own person the anguish of the world's sorrow, its helplessness, its confusion, its sin. He meets the world's foulness with the purity of Jesus; he meets the world's rebellion with the obedience of Jesus; he meets the world's hatred with the love of the sacred heart of Jesus and so takes his part in reversing the sin of the world.[10]

In districts where the night is a time associated with much loneliness, misery, and wrong, a disciplined Christian community praying at times throughout the night would be valuable. The forces of evil will only be defeated at the level of the spiritual warfare of which Thomas Merton writes when he describes the contemplative vocation:[11]

> You just lie there, inert, helpless, alone, in the dark and let yourself be crushed by the inscrutable tyranny of time. The plank bed becomes an altar, and you lie there without trying to understand any longer in what sense you can be called a sacrifice. Outside in the world, where it is night, perhaps there is someone who suddenly sees that something he has done is terrible. He is most unexpectedly sorry and finds himself able to pray.

3. PRIESTHOOD AND SACRAMENTS

Just as this eucharistic action is the pattern of all Christian action, the sharing of this bread the sign for the sharing of

all bread, so this fellowship is the germ of all society redeemed in Christ.   BISHOP JOHN A. T. ROBINSON[12]

The priest who ministers in the drug scene will experience
a terrible sense of sacramental aloneness as he articulates
the prayers of those who cannot pray and feeds on the body
of Christ for those who cannot share it with him. He will
lean very heavily on the group of fellow-Christians whom he
has gathered around him. But a very large part of his
ministry will be spent with those for whom the inner
reality of his life in grace will mean nothing. Yet his
ministry is set within the sacramental life of the Body of
Christ.

The sacramental world exists at the heart of the drug
scene as it does anywhere else. Here, in the mystery of
Baptism, the Christian soul turns his back on the powers
of darkness and is plunged into the waters of liberation and
cleansing. Here, in the Sacrifice of the Mass, the soul loses
itself in the cosmic offering of the Son of Man and shares
in his life. This is the heart of the Christian experience of
life in God, and it may be the priest's joy to guide some
souls out of slavery into the liberation of the sons of God,
to initiate them into the mystery of Christ's dying and
rising. But in reality, whenever the sacrifice is shared, those
who share Christ's suffering in the world also share his life
and are drawn into the fellowship of his Body.

The priest acts too as confessor and spiritual director.
He will certainly find that he hears more "informal confessions" in the bars of pubs, clubs, and coffee bars, in prison
cells, court waiting-rooms, and streets than in the confessional. It is difficult to know in such cases where the seal
of the confessional should be upheld. It seems best to treat
any conversation which is explicitly of a confidential nature
as if it were under the seal, even though technically this is
not so. The priest's responsibility here is very great, for
from the moment that he reveals any fact which has been
told to him in confidence his ministry ceases to be trustworthy and secure. Young people in particular will not feel

that they can rely on him. In principle it is wise, even before speaking to doctors, psychiatrists, and probation officers, to ask the person's permission first. It hardly needs to be emphasized that anything told in the confessional must never be revealed, however grave or terrible it may be.

Two types of problem which will face a priest in his role of confessor must be referred to briefly. The first is that, in the drug field as in the whole field of mental illness, the priest will find himself in contact with people for whom "sin" and "guilt" are often confused, and where it is hard to draw a meaningful distinction between voluntary and involuntary behaviour. The priest, as confessor, is concerned solely with the absolution of *actual* sins consciously committed. He is not there to diagnose the movements of the unconscious, nor is he trained to do so. It is probably best, in cases where actual sin is uncertain, to err on the side of leniency, but there are some souls who need fairly strict guidance and direction if they are to make any progress at all.

The second problem concerns the moral status of drug-taking. There is no sin about drug-taking as such. The ingestion of a chemical substance into the body, itself a series of chemical substances, is in itself neither good nor bad. The Christian must be very careful not to fall into the Manichean heresy of regarding the body as evil and looking with disapproval on the physical components of the world. Nothing which goes into the body can defile a man (Mat. 15.11 ff.): this is a basic biblical principle. The taking of drugs under strict medical control does not concern the priest. The point at which moral questions arise lies in the field of non-therapeutic drug use. What attitude should the priest take here?

First, if the person concerned is an addict, whatever the cause of his addiction might be, he must be treated as a sick person. Whatever may be the rights and wrongs of his becoming an addict, at this moment in time his dependence on drugs is a physiological and psychological fact and must be accepted. Secondly, the priest must try to lead the person to view his drug-taking responsibly. He needs therefore to point to the Christian teaching that the body is the temple of the Holy Spirit (1 Cor. 6.19) and is formed in the image of God. If the person has come to the point of confession, one can assume a degree of Christian commitment. The priest has no authority or right to direct a non-Christian, although he may advise him if his advice is sought: but his commission is to feed the flock of Christ within his Body. Christian drug-takers will need very careful spiritual guidance. It should not be difficult, in principle, to advise those whose drug use has reached the point of chronic abuse with harmful effects such as were described in Part One of this book. The difficulties may arise, generally in the case of cannabis, where the young Christian genuinely sees nothing sinful in his use of the drug for pleasure. In such cases, the priest may *advise* him, as a personal opinion, that it is unwise to continue, and may feel the need to avert a forthcoming casualty: he has no right, as a priest, to treat such drug use as *per se* sinful. If the person sincerely, after prayer and reflection, is convinced that he is right, he must not be refused absolution any more than the drinker, the cigarette-smoker, or the taker of snuff.

There remain two aspects of sacramental activity which should be mentioned. First, the laying-on-of-hands and anointing. This sacrament is applicable to drug dependence as to any other illness and the caution and judgement applied elsewhere should be used in this sphere also. The danger of "mechanical" or even "magical" concepts must be avoided. But clearly there is an important place for the use of anointing within the framework of a healing ministry. The addict who is a Christian will, of course, be guided through prayer and sacrament, and anointing will take place in this context. The addict who is not a Christian but who expresses faith in God of some kind can also be anointed, and this may indeed have a profound spiritual impact upon him.

Secondly, the ministry of exorcism or the binding of evil powers. This ministry needs to be studied very carefully indeed before any action is taken, and there is clear danger of irresponsible use of these spiritual powers. Briefly, the theology of exorcism is based on the New Testament teaching about the existence of non-human evil forces and the triumph of Christ over them. It is important to remember that exorcism of persons was a normal routine action for all candidates for baptism and has been an element in baptismal rites since the time of Hippolytus. The emphasis is on the liberation of creation and individuals within it from disorder and distortion. The act of exorcism consists of the recital of a formula, accompanied by some action such as the sprinkling of holy water, the sign of the cross, or (as in the Paschal blessing of the font) a deep directed breath. The more specific exorcism applied to a case of demonic possession can only be performed by a priest under the express authority of the bishop, and it should not take place except after long medical and psychological investigation. The short exorcism, however, which is of "every unclean spirit", could certainly be used in cases where the influence of uncertain evil forces was perceived. It is dangerous to assume that addicted persons or any other sick individuals are necessarily "possessed": it is evident, on the other hand, that, like the rest of us, they share the consequences of evil in the world, and it would seem right to accompany prayer and sacramental acts with a prayer for their liberation from the influence of any adverse power.

The priest in the drug scene acts as one mediator of the life of Christ in his Body the Church. He is present both to heal and, by prayer and sacrament, to draw the scene within the love of Christ. It is a scene characterized at many points by loneliness and desolation, but so is the spiritual way itself. The priest's privilege is to guide the children of God until they "expire into the eternal namelessness, where we are lost . . . in a pathless unknown darkness".

There are we all with God, without distinction, beatitude
infinite and simple. There are we lost, drowned, and liquefied
into an unknown darkness. This is the highest degree of life
and of death.[13]

Notes

Some Useful Addresses

Select Bibliography

Index

Abbreviations

Am. J. Psych.	American Journal of Psychiatry
B.M.J.	British Medical Journal
Brit. J. Add.	British Journal of Addiction
Brit. J. Crim.	British Journal of Criminology
Brit. J. Psych.	British Journal of Psychiatry
Bull. Narc.	Bulletin of Narcotics
Bull. W.H.O.	Bulletin of the World Health Organization
Clin. Pharmacol. and Ther.	Clinical Pharmacology and Therapeutics
Int. J. Add.	International Journal of the Addictions
I.T.	International Times
J.A.M.A.	Journal of the American Medical Assn.
J. Coll. G.P.	Journal of the College of General Practitioners
J. Ment. Sci.	Journal of Mental Science
J. Offender Ther.	Journal of Offender Therapy
J. Pharmacol. and Exper. Ther.	Journal of Pharmacology and Experimental Therapeutics
Proc. R.S.M.	Proceedings of the Royal Society of Medicine

Others are given in full or are self-explanatory.

Notes

CHAPTER 1

1. Cited I. Pierce James, *Brit. J. Add.* 62 (1967), 391
2. See Isidor Chein, Donald L. Gerard, Robert S. Lee, and Eva Rosenfeld, *Narcotics, Delinquency, and Social Policy. The Road to H* (1964), 335
3. World Health Organization Technical Report Series, No. 407, *W.H.O. Expert Committee on Drug Dependence: 16th Report* (1969), 6
4. See further Anthony Horden, "Psychopharmacology: Some Historical Considerations" in C. R. B. Joyce (ed.) *Psychopharmacology: Dimensions and Perspectives* (1968), 95–148
5. I owe this distinction to the British Medical Association's "Report of the Working Party on Amphetamine Preparations" (MS. 1968), para. 1.12
6. See C. F. Essig, "Addiction to non-barbiturate sedative and tranquillizing drugs", *Clin. Pharm. and Ther.* 5 (1964), 336; ibid. "Newer sedative drugs that can cause states of intoxication and dependence of barbiturate type", *J.A.M.A.* 196:8 (1966), 714–17; L. E. Hollister, F. P. Motzenbecker, and R. O. Degan, "Withdrawal reactions from chlordiazepoxide (Librium)", *Psychopharm.* 2:1 (1961), 63–68
7. Cf. Brian Inglis, *Drugs, Doctors, and Disease* (1965), on side-effects of antibiotics and tranquillizers. P. C. Elmes and O. L. Wade, in a study of 47 advertisements in *B.M.J.* 20 October 1962, concluded that 26 made excessive claims and 7 did not mention serious side effects (Inglis, 88). L. E. Hollister "Adverse reactions to phenothiazines", *J.A.M.A.* 189:4 (1964), 143–5 discusses adverse behavioural reactions but points out that clinical addiction is unknown.
8. N. B. Eddy, H. Halbach, H. Isbell, and M. H. Seevers, "Drug dependence: its significance and characteristics", *Bull. W.H.O.* 32:5 (1965), 722
9. *W.H.O. Technical Report Series*, No. 287 (1964), 5
10. I shall use "addict" (rather than "drug dependent person") and "addictive" (rather than "productive of physical dependence") for simplicity's sake. But the qualifications mentioned here need to be borne in mind.

11. Tanzi, *Textbook of Mental Disease* (1909), cited I. Pierce James *Brit. J. Crim.* April 1969, 108

12. Ihno J. Bensussan, *Opium* (Paris, 1946)

13. James, op. cit. 108

14. P. T. D'Orban, "Heroin Dependence and Delinquency in Women" (MS. 1969) (in the press)

15. *Report to the United Nations by Her Majesty's Government of the United Kingdom and Northern Ireland on the Working of the International Treaties on Narcotic Drugs 1955*, para. 35

16. E. M. Brooke and M. M. Glatt, *Medicine, Science, and the Law*, October 1964, 277

17. W. Willcox, *British Journal of Inebriety* 31 (1934), 131

18. J. Lockett, 1952, cited B. G. Adams. *J. Coll. Gen. Practit.* 12 (1966), 24

19. For further details, see G. R. Todd (ed.) *Extra Pharmacopoeia: Martindale* (1967 ed.), 180-201

20. See G. B. Adams, "Patients receiving barbiturates in an urban general practice", *J. Coll. Gen. Practit.* 12 (1966), 24-31

21. M. M. Glatt "The abuse of barbiturates in the United Kingdom", *Bull. Narc.* 14:2 (1962), 19-38

22. P. H. Blachly, "Procedure for withdrawal of barbiturates" *Am. J. Psych.* 120 (1964), 894-5

23. William Burroughs, *The Naked Lunch* (1968), 281

24. See, for example, the two studies by Essig, op. cit; Ian M. Grant, "Drug Habituation in an Urban General Practice", *Practitioner* 202 (1969), 428-30; Hollister etc., op. cit.

25. G. B. Adams, op. cit., 29

CHAPTER 2

1. Ministry of Health *Report for the Year 1954*, Part 2 (1955)

2. G. A. Alles, *J. Pharmacol. and Exp. Ther.* 32 (1927), 121: 47 (1933), 339

3. D. Young and W. B. Scoville, *Med. Clin. N. Amer.* 22 (1938), 637

4. R. R. Monroe and H. J. Drell, *J.A.M.A.* 135 (1947), 909

5. See K. Morimoto, "The problem of the abuse of amphetamines in Japan", *Bull. Narc.* 9:3 (1957), 8-12

6. S. Taletsu "Methylamphetamine Psychosis", *Folia Psychiat. Neurol Japan.* Suppl. 7 (1963), 377-80

7. See Nils Bejerot, "An Epidemic of Phemetrazine Dependence—Epidemiological and Clinical Aspects", in C. W. M. Wilson (ed.) *The Pharmacological and Epidemiological Aspects of Adolescent Drug Dependence* (1968), 55-66

8. P. H. Connell, *Amphetamine Psychosis* (1958)

9. See bibliography

10. British Medical Association, "Report of the Working Party on Amphetamine Preparations" MS. 1968, para. 10.2

11. For fuller details see G. R. Todd (ed.) *Extra Pharmacopoeia: Martindale* (1967 ed.) 97–109, and *MIMS* (Monthly Index of Medical Specialities) monthly.

12. BMA Report, op. cit., para. 7:13

13. R. E. Yoss and D. D. Daly, *Med. Clin. N. Amer.* 44 (1960), 953

14. S. Brandon and D. Smith, *J. Coll. Gen. Pract.* 5 (1962), 604

15. See, for example, D. S. Bell and W. H. Threthowan, "Amphetamine Addiction", *J. Nerv. and Ment. Diseases*, 133 (1961), 489–496; John Evans, "Psychosis and Addiction to Phenmetrazine (Preludin)", *Lancet*, 22 August 1959, 152–5; L. G. Kiloh and S. Brandon "Habituation and Addiction to Amphetamines", *B.M.J.* 7 July 1962, 40–3; Frederick Lemere "The Danger of Amphetamine Dependency", *Am. J. Psych.* 123 (1966), 569–72; Ian Oswald and V. R. Thacore "Amphetamine and Phenmetrazine Addiction", *B.M.J.* 17 August 1963, 427–31; J. A. Sours, "Addiction to Daprisal", *J.A.M.A.* 205 (1968), 940

16. Connell, op. cit., 71

17. Kiloh and Brandon, op. cit.

18. D. Hawks, M. Mitcheson, A. Ogborne, and G. Edwards, "The abuse of methylamphetamine", MS. Addiction Research Unit, Institute of Psychiatry, 1969. A shortened version of this paper appeared in *B.M.J.* 21 June 1969, 715–21. References made here are to the MS.

19. Lemere, op. cit., 570; Taletsu, op. cit., 377–80

20. I. P. James, *Lancet*, 1968, 916. M. M. Glatt, ibid., 215

21. Personal communication, CIBA Laboratories, 18 October 1968

22. See, for example, T. C. McCormick, Jr., and T. W. McNeel, "Acute psychosis and Ritalin abuse", *Texas State J. Med.* 59 (1963), 99–100

23. See Nils Bejerot, op. cit.; John Evans, op. cit.; Oswald and Thacore, op. cit.; J. B. Randell, "Euphoriant Effects of 'Preludin'", *B.M.J.* 31 August 1957, 508–9

24. Hawks *et al.*, op. cit., 27

25. Marie Nyswander in Ernest Harms (ed.) *Drug Addiction in Youth* (1965), 126

26. M. M. Glatt, *Brit. J. Add.* 63 (1968), 115

27. C. F. Essig, ("Addiction to non-barbiturate sedative and tranquillizing drugs", *Clin. Pharmacol. and Ther.* 5 (1964), 336) claimed that glutethimide "can induce intoxication and physical dependence in both animal and man". See also his "Newer sedative drugs that can cause states of intoxication and dependence of barbiturate type", *J.A.M.A.* 196:8 (1966), 714–17

28. See R. de Alarcon, letter in *B.M.J.* 11 January 1969

29. M. M. Glatt, op. cit., noted that "we have come successively across cases of psychological dependence on methylpentynol, glutethimide, methylprylone, dichloralphenazone, and methaqualone shortly after their coming on the market", but stresses that "the risk of leading to dependence seems . . . on the whole somewhat less than with barbiturates".

30. P. A. L. Chapple, "Report on Second Year's Work of the Chelsea Centre", MS. 1969, 4

31. G. R. Burston, *Practitioner*, 199 (1967), 343

32. A. A. H. Lawson and S. S. Brown, *B.M.J.* 10 December 1966, 1455. See also their article "Acute Methaqualone (Mandrax) poisoning", *Scot. Med. J.* 12 (1967), 63-8

33. J. P. W. Young, letter, *B.M.J.* 4 February 1967, 301

34. *Lancet*, 1966, 803

35. For details on Mandrax abuse see the valuable booklet *Mandrax* issued by Roussel Laboratories

CHAPTER 3

1. *Drug Addiction, Report of the Interdepartmental Committee* (1961), para. 24

2. I. Pierce James, *Brit. J. Crim.* April 1969, 111

3. See *Report to the United Nations by Her Majesty's Government of the United Kingdom of Great Britain and Northern Ireland on the Working of the International Treaties on Narcotic Drugs*, 1967

4. Ibid., 1968

5. Ibid., 1964, para. 40

6. *Drug Addiction, Second Report of the Interdepartmental Committee*, 1965

7. *Report to the United Nations, etc.* 1965, para. 37

8. Ibid., para. 42

9. Ibid., 1967, paras. 33, 37

10. Op. cit., paras. 11-12

11. G. B. Oppenheim, letter, *Lancet*, 7 June 1969. In a study of sources of drugs of 66 addicts in Brixton Prison in the first few months of 1969, it was found that 57 per cent used clinics, 20 per cent general practitioners, and 22 per cent illicit sources only. (I. P. James, personal communication)

12. Ibid.

13. See *The Problem of Narcotic Drugs in Hong Kong* (Hong Kong, 1962)

14. Alan Bestic, *Daily Mirror*, 7 May 1969

15. See *The Rehabitation of Drug Addicts*. Report of the Advisory Committee on Drug Dependence (1969) Appendix B.

16. See, for example, Adele Kosviner *et al.*, "Heroin use in a provincial town", *Lancet*, 1 June 1968, 1189–92; R. de Alarcon, "The spread of heroin abuse in a community", *Bull. Narc.* 21:3 (1969), 17–22

17. de Alarcon, op. cit., 17

18. T. H. Bewley, O. Ben-Arie, and I. P. James, *B.M.J.*, 23 March 1968, 725–6

19. I. P. James, *Brit. J. Add.* 62 (1967), 391–8

20. T. H. Bewley, *et al.*, op. cit., 726

21. Julius Merry, *Brit. J. Add.* 63 (1968), 247–50

22. Charles Winick, *Current History*, June 1967, 349–54

23. Cf. for example, Alasdair MacIntyre, *New Society*. 5 December 1968, 848: "what involves the cannabis taker and the heroin addict in a common subculture seems to be primarily the illegality of both".

24. I. P. James, *Brit. J. Crim.* April 1969, 115

25. Ibid.

26. Efren Ramirez, "A Comprehensive Plan for the Management of the Addiction Problem in New York City based on the Puerto Rican Experience", MS. 1968, 2

27. Ibid.

28. William Burroughs, *Junkie* (1966 ed.), 12

29. J. H. Willis, *Drug Dependence* (1969), 31

30. Alfred R. Lindesmith, *Opiate Addiction* (1968 ed.)

31. A. Wikler and R. W. Rasor. *Am. J. Med.* 14 (1953), 566

32. A. Wikler, "Conditioning factors in opiate addiction and withdrawal", in D. M. Wilner and G. G. Kassebaum (ed.), *Narcotics* (1965)

33. Lindesmith, op. cit., 181

34. W. J. Kirkpatrick, "The Drug Dependency Problem", MS. 1968

35. L. Kolb, *Mental Hygiene*, 9 (1925), 699, claims that "the intensity of pleasure produced by opiates is in direct proportion to the degree of psychopathy of the person who becomes an addict". See also his *Drug Addiction* (1962)

36. M. M. Glatt, in C. W. M. Wilson (ed.) *The Pharmacological and Epidemiological Aspects of Adolescent Drug Dependence* (1968), 172

37. W. J. Kirkpatrick, op. cit.

38. J. H. Willis, *Nursing Times*, 14 April 1967, 474

39. J. H. Willis, *Drug Dependence* (1969), 71–2

40. M. Hoffman, *Comprehensive Psychology* 5 (1964), 262

41. Isidor Chein, Donald L. Gerard, Robert S. Lee, and Eva Rosenfeld, *Narcotics, Delinquency, and Social Policy. The Road to H.* (1964), 218f

42. P. T. D'Orban, "Heroin Dependence and Delinquency in Women", MS. 1969, 6

43. Ibid., 16

44. See James, *Brit. J. Crim.* April 1969, 113; T. H. Bewley and J. H. Willis, letter, *Times*, 16 January 1969

45. James, op. cit., 115–24

46. See V. P. Dole and Marie Nyswander, "A medical treatment for diacetylmorphine (heroin) addiction", *J.A.M.A.* 193:8. (1965), 646–50; Nathan B. Eddy, "The chemotherapy of drug dependence", *Brit. J. Add.* 61 (1966), 155–67; Gertrude Samuels, "Drug against Drug", *New Society*, 17 October 1968, 553–4

47. See Leon Brill and J. H. Jaffe, "The relevancy of some newer American treatment approaches for England", *Brit. J. Add.* 62 (1967), 375–86; Alfred M. Freedman and Max Fink, "Basic concepts and use of cyclazocine in the treatment of narcotic addiction", *Brit. J. Add.* 63 (1968), 59–69; J. H. Jaffe and Leon Brill, "Cyclazocine, a long-acting narcotic antagonist", *Int. J. Add.* January 1966, 99–123; W. R. Martin, C. W. Gorodetsky, and T. K. McClane, "An experimental study in the treatment of narcotic addicts with cyclazocine", *Clin. Pharmacol. and Ther.* 7:4 (1966), 455–65

48. See Geoffrey Knight, "The approach of the neuro-surgeon to the treatment of drug addiction". MS. 1969; ibid., "Chronic depression and drug addiction treated by stereotactic surgery", *Nursing Times*, 8 May 1969, 583–6

49. See I. G. Thomson and N. H. Rathod, "Aversion therapy for heroin dependence", *Lancet*, 17 August 1968, 382–4

50. Efren Ramirez, op. cit.

51. See David Deitch and Daniel Casriel, *The Role of the Ex-Addict in Treatment of Addiction* (reprinted from *Federal Probation*) (1967); Dan L. Garnett, "Synanon: The Communiversity", *The Humanist* (U.S.A.) September-October 1965, 185–9; L. Yablonsky, *The Tunnel Back* (1965)

52. *The Rehabilitation of Drug Addicts*, op. cit., para. 17

CHAPTER 4

1. From a lecture given in 1968

2. L. Lewin, *Phantastica* (1931), 109

3. E. R. Bloomquist, *Marijuana* (1968). The word "hashish" has been associated, probably wrongly, with the Hashishen (Assassin) sects founded by Hasan-ibn-al Sabbah around A.D. 1090

4. C. Creighton, "On indications of the hashish-vice in the Old Testament", *Janus*, 8 (1903), 241–6, 297–303

5. Bloomquist, op. cit., 19

6. R. N. Chopra and I. C. Chopra, *Drug Addiction with Special Reference to India* (1965), 172f

7. *Daily Mail*, 28 February 1938

8. *Daily Mail*, 9 September 1948

9. *Sunday Dispatch*, 12 September 1948

10. *Evening News*, 18 September 1949

11. *Sunday Dispatch*, 16 April 1950; *People*, 19 November 1950

12. United Nations, *Summary of Annual Reports of Governments for 1950* (1952), 32f

13. *Daily Mail*, 28 March 1952

14. M. P. Banton, *The Coloured Quarter* (1955), 196–7

15. A. B. Toklas, *Cook Book* (Penguin, 1961 ed.) 306: "haschich fudge". She refers to "*canibus* sativa" which she thinks may be difficult to obtain!

15a. T. H. Bewley, *Bull. Narc.* 18:4 (1966), 5

16. See *Cannabis: Report by the Advisory Committee on Drug Dependence* (1968), para. 35

16a. *Daily Mail*, 17 April 1963

17. See, for example, Sidney Cohen, "Psychotomimetic Agents", *Annual Review of Pharmacology*, 7 (1967), 301–8

18. The evidence for this is virtually overwhelming and the literature immense. Thus S. Allentuck and K. M. Bowman, *Am. J. Psych.* 99 (1942), 249: "The psychic habituation to marihuana is not as strong as to tobacco or alcohol." William Burroughs, *Junkie* (1966), 30: ". . . positively not habit-forming". Nathan B. Eddy, H. Halbach, H. Isbell, and M. H. Seevers, *Bull. W.H.O.* 32:5 (1965), 728: "Even during long and continuous administration, no evidence of the development of physical dependence can be detected." *Drug Addiction, Report of the Interdepartmental Committee* (1961) para. 54: "Cannabis is not a drug of addiction. It is an intoxicant." *J.A.M.A.* 201 (1967), 369: "No physical dependence or tolerance has been demonstrated." D. M. Louria, *Nightmare Drugs* (1966), 32: "It is non-addicting, and does not produce physical illness of deterioration in the user, at least if smoked in moderation." *The Marihuana Problem in the City of New York* (Mayor's Committee on Marihuana, 1944), 25: "The practice of smoking marihuana does not lead to addiction in the medical sense of the word." Panama Canal Zone Governor's Committee Report in *The Military Surgeon*, November 1933, 274: "There is no evidence that marihuana as grown here is a 'habit-forming' drug in the sense in which the term is applied to alcohol, opium, colavic, etc., or that it has any appreciably deleterious influence on the individual using it." H. B. Murphy, *Bull. Narc.* 15 (1963), 15–23 on the current literature. E. M. Schur, *Narcotic Addiction in Britain and America* (1963), 33: "It

should not be considered a truly addictive drug; there seems little justification for the term 'marijuana addiction' which one sometimes encounters." Charles Winick in E. Harms (ed.), *Drug Addiction in Youth* (1964), 22: "There is some reason to suspect that habituation to marijuana may be less compelling than to alcohol." J. M. Watt in G. E. W. Wolstenholme and J. Knight (ed.), *Hashish: Its Chemistry and Pharmacology* (1964), 54: "Cannabis does not produce a real addiction. It does not give rise to biological dependence and withdrawal symptoms, neither does it establish a strong craving as in tobacco smoking or indulgence in alcohol." See J. M. Watt, "Drug Dependence of Hashish Type" in ibid., 54-66. This is only a small selection from the literature, and more articles and fuller references are given in a separate Bibliography obtainable from the author

19. See, for example, P. A. L. Chapple, *Brit. J. Add.* 61 (1966), 279; J. S. Madden, letter, *Times*, 14 January 1969; J. M. Watt, op. cit.

20. *Cannabis*, op. cit., para. 29

21. *Report of the Indian Hemp Drugs Commission 1893-4* (7 vols. 1897), Ch. 10, para. 498; Ch. 11, para. 510

22. *The Marihuana Problem in the City of New York* (Mayor's Committee on Marihuana, 1944) 218

23. See B. C. Bose, A. Q. Saifi, and A. W. Bhagwat, "Studies on pharmacological actions of Cannabis Indica. Part 3", *Arch. Int. Pharmacodyn.* 147:1-2 (1946), 291-7

24. L. Goldman and A. Gilman, *The Pharmacological Basis of Therapeutics* (1956), 170-7

25. A. T. Weil, N. E. Zinberg, and J. M. Nelsen, *Science*, 162 (1968), 1241

26. Op. cit., para. 30

27. Ibid., para. 62

28. A. T. Weil, N. T. Zinberg, and J. M. Nelsen, "Clinical and psychological effects of marihuana in man", *Science*, 162 (1968), 1234-42. See also N. Zinberg and A. Weil, "Cannabis: the first controlled experiment", *New Society*, 16 January 1969, 84-6

29. See A. H. Henderson and D. J. Pugsley, "Collapse after intravenous injection of hashish", *B.M.J.* 27 July 1968, 229-30

30. W. H. McGlothlin in David Solomon (ed.), *The Marihuana Papers* (1966), 456

31. A. R. Lindesmith, *The Addict and the Law* (1965), 224

32. C. W. M. Wilson and A. Linken in *The Pharmocological and Epidemiological Aspects of Adolescent Drug Dependence* (1968), 119

33. Though Zinberg *et al.* point out (*Science*, 162 (1968), 1235) that "THC has not been established as the sole determinant of marihuana's activity."

34. H. Isbell *et al.*, "Effects of $(-)\Delta^9$—Trans-Tetrahydro-Cannabinol in Man", *Psychopharmacologia* (Berlin), 11 (1967), 184–8
35. See Lawrence Lipton, *The Holy Barbarians* (1962), 156
36. William Burroughs, *Guardian*, 7 July 1969
37. Charles Winick and Marie Nyswander, *Am. J. Orthopsych*, 31 (1961), 622
38. M. M. Glatt, *Brit. J. Add.* 64 (1969), 111
39. *Hapt*, 1968, no page number or date
40. *British Pharmaceutical Codex* (1949), 197–201. The codex observes: "Cannabis depresses first the higher critical faculties and later the perceptive sensory and motor areas of the cerebrum. In some persons, particularly orientals, it produces a type of inebriation with a feeling of pleasurable excitement and some mental confusion, fantastic or exotic hallucinations, and a loss of the ability to estimate time and space; later, decreased sensitiveness to touch and pain, as well as muscular lethargy and relaxation, precede the onset of a comatose sleep in which respiration is slowed and the pupils are dilated. In other persons it may cause only lethargy with some irritability of temper. Cannabis is a habit-forming drug and habitués often become insane; amongst orientals it is taken as a drink or conserve or smoked in pipes or cigarettes under the name of charas, ganjah, guaza, bhang, and hashish; in South Africa, it is smoked under the name of dagga, and in Mexico and Brazil it is the active ingredient of marijuana cigarettes. Cannabis is too unreliable in action to be of value in therapeutics as a cerebral sedative or narcotic and its former use in mania and nervous disorders has been abandoned."
41. J. Kabelik, *Bull. Narc.* 12:3 (1960), 5
42. A. D. Macdonald, *Nature*, 147 (1941), 168
43. Elizabeth Tylden, *Cannabis Taking in England* (reprinted from *Newcastle Med. J.* 30:6), 1968
44. O. Moraes Andrade, *Bull. Narc.* 16:4 (1964), 27
45. Elizabeth Tylden, letter, *B.M.J.* 26 August 1967, cf. also P. Dally, letter, ibid., 5 August 1967
46. Elizabeth Tylden, "Questions About Cannabis", MS. 1968
47. See Ahmed Benabud, "Psycho-sociological aspects of the cannabis situation in Morocco", *Bull. Narc.* 9:4 (1957), 1–16; I. C. Chopra and R. N. Chopra, "The Use of the Cannabis drugs in India", ibid., 9:1 (1957), 4–29; T. Asuni, "Socio-psychiatric problems of cannabis in Nigeria", ibid. 16:2 (1964), 17–28
48. Benabud, op. cit., 6, 10ff.
49. Chopra and Chopra, op. cit., 24. But R. N. Chopra, G. S. Chopra, and I. C. Chopra, *Indian J. Med. Research*, 30:1 (1942), 155 put the rate of insanity among Indian cannabis smokers at 1·93 per cent, not above the general population

50. Asuni, op. cit.

51. Benabud, op. cit.

52. Chopra and Chopra, op. cit., 24. Cf. also R. N. Chopra and I. C. Chopra. *Drug Addiction with Special Reference to India* (1965), 177

53. *Report*, op. cit., ch. 10, para. 498

54. *S. African Med. J.* (Editorial), 25:17 (1951), 284–6

55. Howard S. Becker, in Charles Hollander (ed.), *Background Papers on Student Drug Involvement* (1967), 78

56. Ibid., 77

57. S. Allentuck and K. M. Bowman, *Am. J. Psych.* 99 (1942), 249. Cf. also Sidney Cohen, *Annual Review of Pharmacology*, 7 (1967), 315: ". . . an occasional psychotic reaction particularly in the unstable personality". H. B. Murphy, *Bull. Narc.* 15 (1963), 22: "It probably produces a specific psychosis, but this must be quite rare, since the prevalence of psychosis in cannabis users is only doubtfully higher than the prevalence in general populations." Charles Winick in E. Harms (ed.), *Drug Addiction in Youth* (1965), 24: "It is very unlikely that marihuana will itself lead to a psychosis in a person who is well integrated. The extent to which marihuana triggers an already latent psychotic condition or creates it, for however brief a period, is not clear." William Burroughs, *Junkie* (1966), 31: "Weed psychosis corresponds more or less to delirium tremens and quickly disappears when the drug is withdrawn." W. E. Mayer-Gross, E. Slater, and M. Roth, *Clinical Psychiatry* (1954), cited in D. Solomon (ed.), *The Marihuana Papers* (1966), 466: "The chronic hashish psychoses described by earlier observers have proved to be cases of schizophrenia complicated by symptoms of cannabis intoxication." Walter Bromberg, *J.A.M.A.* 113 (1939), 7–8: "The inner relationship between cannabis (marihuana) and the onset of a functional psychotic state is not always clear. The inner reaction to somatic sensation seems vital. Such reactions consisted of panic states which disappeared as soon as the stimulus (effects of the drug) faded." D. M. Louria in C. W. M. Wilson (ed.), *The Pharmacological Epidemiological Aspects of Adolescent Drug Dependence* (1968), 89: [Moderate use has] "no valid statistical connection either with criminality or psychosis".

58. *Cannabis*, op. cit., para. 69. See also Appendix 1 (40–57)

59. In Ibid., Appendix 1, 50–1

60. Becker, op. cit., 72

61. Charles Winick in E. Harms (ed.), *Drug Addiction in Youth* (1965), 24

62. H. Isbell *et al.*, "Studies in Tetrahydrocannabinol", 1968, 4844

63. Ibid. Cf. also C. J. Miras, *Marihuana and Hashish* (1968), 6: "The symptoms in hashish intoxication depend on the number of the 'active THC' introduced into the organism and not on the number of cigarettes *per se*."

64. C. R. B. Joyce, letter, *New Society*, 30 January 1969, 181

65. Cf. D. M. Louria, *Nightmare Drugs* (1966), 65: "Although it is true that most heroin users had prior experiences with marijuana, it is also true that the overwhelming majority of those who try marijuana on one or more occasions never turn either to heroin or to stronger hallucinogenic agents."

66. N. B. Eddy, H. Halbach, H. Isbell, and M. H. Seevers, *Bull. W.H.O.* 32:5 (1965), 729

67. Erich Goode, "Multiple Drug Use Among Marijuana Smokers", MS. 1969. 16

68. *Cannabis*, op. cit., para. 49

69. Adele Kosviner et alia, *Lancet*, 1 June 1968, 1192: "Although all our subjects had tried soft drugs before using heroin, we found no evidence to suggest any necessary progression from soft to hard drugs."

70. *Blenheim Project: Detached Social Work with Young Drifters in London 2nd Annual Report* (1966), 3: "So far as our group of young drug-takers is concerned, there is little evidence as yet to support the escalation theory of movement from 'soft' to 'hard' drugs."

71. P. T. D'Orban, "Heroin Dependence and Delinquency in Women", MS. 1969 (in the press)

CHAPTER 5

1. Timothy Leary, Ralph Metzner, and Richard Alpert, *The Psychedelic Experience* (1966), 14

2. H. Osmond, *Ann. N.Y. Academy of Science*, 66 (1957), 418

3. Aldous Huxley, *Heaven and Hell* (1956), 63

4. See Havelock Ellis, "Mescal, a new artificial Paradise", in *Annual Report, Smithsonian Institution*, 1897, 537–48

5. G. T. Stockings, "A clinical study of the mescaline psychosis with special reference to the mechanism of the genesis of schizophrenic and other psychotic states", *J. Ment. Sci.* 86 (1940), 29–47. See also Max Rinkel and Herman C. B. Denber, *Chemical Concepts of Psychosis* (1958).

6. Cited by D. M. Louria in C. W. M. Wilson (ed.), *The Pharmacological and Epidemiological Aspects of Adolescent Drug Dependence* (1968), 83

7. Frank Lake, *Clinical Theology* (1966), 697

8. See, for example, T. M. Ling and J. Buckman, "The use of lysergic acid in individual psychotherapy", *Proc. R.S.M.* 53 (1960), 43–5; Richard Crocket, R. A. Sandison, and Alexander Walk, *Hallucinogenic Drugs and their Psychotherapeutic Use* (1963)

9. D. M. Louria, op. cit., 86

10. Reginald G. Smart and Karen Bateman, "Unfavourable reactions to LSD", *Canadian Med. Assoc. J.* 97 (1967), 1214–21

11. Sidney Cohen, "A classification of LSD complications", *Psychosomatics*, 7 (1966), 182–6

12. Leary, Metzner, and Alpert, op. cit., 135

13. M. E. Jarvik in R. C. DeBold and R. C. Leaf, *LSD, Man and Society* (1969), 189

14. R. A. Sandison, A. M. Spencer, and J. D. A. Whitehouse, *J. Ment. Sci.* 100 (1954), 498

15. See Joe K. Adams "Psychosis: 'Experimental' and Real" in Gunther M. Weil, Ralph Metzner, and Timothy Leary (ed.), *The Psychedelic Reader* (1965), 65–88

16. Leary, Metzner, and Alpert, op. cit., 11

17. Allan Y. Cohen, "LSD and the student: approaches to educational strategies", MS. California, 1967, 11

18. See M. M. Cohen, K. Hirschhorn, and W. A. Frosch, "In vivo and in vitro chromosomal damage induced by LSD-25", *N. Eng. J. Med.* 277:20 (1967), 1043–9; Takashi Kato and L. F. Jarvik, "LSD-25 and genetic damage", *Diseases of the Nervous System*, 30 (1969), 42–6; R. G. Smart and K. Bateman, "The chromosomal and teratogenic effects of lysergic acid diethylamide", *Canadian Med. Assoc. J.*, 99 (1968), 805–10

19. D. M. Louria in Spring 1967 observed "some evidence of a reduction in LSD abuse in areas in which its use has been endemic" (in DeBold and Leaf, op. cit., 37). In Britain the peak period for LSD abuse was the freaky summer of 1967

20. S. H. Snyder, L. Faillace, and L. Hollister, "2,5-dimethoxy-4-methyl-amphetamine (STP): a new hallucinogenic drug", *Science* 158 (1967), 670

21. Ibid. See also L. E. Hollister, M. F. Macnicol, and H. K. Gillespie, "An hallucinogenic amphetamine analog (DOM) in man", *Psychopharmacologia* (Berlin), 14 (1969), 62–73

22. See A. T. Shulgin, "3 methoxy-4,5-methylenedioxy amphetamine, a new psychotominetic agent", *Nature* 14 March 1964

23. See H. Fabing, "On going berserk: a neurochemical enquiry", *Am. J. Psych.* 113 (1956), 409–15

24. Louria, in DeBold and Leaf, op. cit., 41

CHAPTER 6

1. Cited in John Rosevear, *Pot, A Handbook of Marihuana* (1967), 9
2. See Lawrence Lipton, *The Holy Barbarians* (1962)
3. See Jack Kerouac, *On The Road* (1962 ed.); *The Dharma Bums* (1962 ed.); *The Scripture of the Golden Eternity* (1960), etc.
4. Lipton, op. cit., 119ff
5. Lipton, op. cit., 156
6. Ibid.
7. C. Winick and M. Nyswander, *Am. J. Orthopsych*, 31 (1961), 622
8. C. Winick, *Social Problems*, 7:3 (1959–60), 240–53
9. M. P. Banton, *The Coloured Quarter* (1955), 196–7
10. D. M. Downes, *The Delinquent Solution* (1966), 135
11. E. M. Schur, *Narcotic Addiction in Britain and America* (1963), 144–6
12. Downes, op. cit., *passim*.
13. "Blessed" from Simon and Garfunkel, *The Sounds of Silence*, LP. C.B.S.
14. Stephen Abrams in George Andrews and Simon Vinkenoog (ed.) *The Book of Grass* (1967), 239
15. *Drug Addiction, Second Report of the Interdepartmental Committee* (1965), para. 40
16. H. M. Holden in *Teenagers and Drugs* (Education pamphlet 1966), 11
17. K. Leech, *The Drug Scene from St Anne's Soho* (1969)
18. Op. cit., para. 40
19. Laurie Little in *The Soho Project Report* (1969), 15
20. Sidney Cohen, *Medical Science*, February 1968, 35
21. Jordan Scher, *Illinois Med. J.* 130 (1966), 456–63
22. P. T. D'Orban, "Heroin Dependence and Delinquency in Women", MS. 1969
23. D. Hawks, M. Mitcheson, A. Ogborne, and G. Edwards, "The Abuse of Methylamphetamine", MS. 1969
24. Cited in *Report of the Committee on Housing in Greater London* (Milner Holland Committee), (1965), 57
25. H. L. Binnie, *The Attitudes to Drugs and Drug Takers of Students at the University and Colleges of Higher Education in an English Midland City* (1969)
26. Sally Trench, *Bury me in My Boots* (1968)
27. Ibid., 163
28. Commune of the Streets, MS., May 1969
29. Ian Henderson, *Guardian*, 20 May 1969
30. *Blenheim Project, Detached Social Work with Young Drifters in London. Second Annual Report, 1966*

31. *The Rink Report 1968-9*, Appendix I, Social Survey by G. A. Batten, 1969

32. Hawks *et al.*, op. cit., 9-12

33. Isidor Chein, Donald L. Gerard, Robert S. Lee, and Eva Rosenfeld. *Narcotics, Delinquency, and Social Policy. The Road to H.* (1964), 372

34. Cf. M. J. Power. "The Re-Integration of the Young Drug-Dependent Person to the Community", MS. 1968

35. W. J. A. Kirkpatrick, *South African Outlook*, June 1969, 101

36. P. T. D'Orban, op. cit.

37. I. P. James, personal communication

38. Ibid.

39. Caroline Coon, "The Hippy and the Psychedelic Scene: the Underground Movement", MS. 1969, 2

40. Frank S. Williams, "Alienation of Youth as Reflected in the Hippie Movement", MS. 1968

41. Richard R. Lingeman, *Drugs from A to Z: A Dictionary* (1969), 77

42. *Gandalf's Garden*, 5 (1969), 9

43. Allan Y. Cohen, *The A.R.E. Journal* (Association for Research and Enlightenment, Virginia, U.S.A.), 3:4 (1968), 26-33

44. Jane de Mendelssohn, *I.T.* 4-17 July 1969, 5

45. Cited in Caroline Coon and Rufus Harris, *The Release Report on Drug Offenders and the Law* (1969), 58-9

46. See, for example, H. J. Freudenberger, "The Drug 'Scene' in Haight-Ashbury, U.S.A.", *Int. J. Offender Therapy*, 13:1 (1969), 13-17; R. Galbis, Paper on the Washington Free Clinic, MS. 1969; David E. Smith and Alan J. Rose, "Observations in the Haight-Ashbury Medical Clinic of San Francisco", *Clinical Paediatrics*, 7:6 (1968), 313-16

47. For instance, *International Times* in August 1968 described a "growing concern on the scene about the widespread use of methedrine"

48. Caroline Coon, MS., op. cit., 2

CHAPTER 7

1. Simon and Garfunkel, "Bleecker Street", from LP *Wednesday Morning, 3 a.m.* (C.B.S.)

2. W. J. A. Kirkpatrick, *South African Outlook*, June 1969, 94

3. Efren Ramirez, "A Comprehensive Plan for the Management of the Addiction Problem in New York City based on the Puerto Rican Experience", MS. 1968

4. Anton Wallich-Clifford, *The Simon Scene* (1968), 18-19

5. Gordon Matthews, *Case Conference*, 15:9 (1969), 358

6. Bruce Kenrick, *Come Out The Wilderness* (1965), 155

7. I have followed the very detailed list of signs in N. H. Rathod, R. de Alarcon, and I. G. Thomson, "Signs of heroin usage detected by drug users and their parents", *Lancet*, 30 December 1967, 1411–14

8. See George Birdwood, *The Willing Victim: A Parents' Guide to Drug Abuse* (1969), 191–3, for an excellent brief account for the layman on "First-aid in cases of overdosage"

9. See Peter Cooper, *Poisoning by Drugs and Chemicals* (1958); Henry Matthew and A. A. H. Lawson, *Treatment of Common Acute Poisonings* (1967)

10. C. R. B. Joyce in S. Rose (ed.), *Chemical and Biological Warfare* (1968), 40

11. B.M.A. "Report of the Working Party on Amphetamine Preparations", MS. 1968, para. 6:18

12. Rink Report, "The Experimental Project with Unattached Young People", MS. 1968, 17

13. *The Rehabilitation of Drug Addicts:* Report of the Advisory Committee on Drug Dependence (1968), para. 17

14. Ibid., paras. 19, 38

15. Ministry of Health Circular H.M. (67) 183, *The Rehabilitation and Care of Heroin Addicts*, 15 November 1967

16. See W. H. Kyle (ed.) *Healing through Counselling* (1964)

17. Percy Mason, "The Mother of the Addict", *Psychol. Quarterly Suppl.* 32 (1958), 189–99 refers to "the controlling, overpowering, overprotecting, guilt ridden and unhappy women". "She is encountered with such regularity and consistency as to preclude coincidence and to make her assume causal, although not exclusive, importance." (197)

18. "Ash Wednesday", in T. S. Eliot, *Selected Poems*, Faber, 1964, 93

19. David Wilkerson, *The Cross and the Switchblade* (1964)

20. Alistair Cox, Rod Moore, and Carol Lewis, "Work Among Drug Dependents", *Vanguard*, August 1969, 5–6, 42

21. For a good outline of the evangelical approach to the scene, see Frank W. Wilson, *Microscope on Bondage* (1968). Most of the evangelical writing, however, is highly uninformative and marked by factual errors throughout. See, for example, Keith Bill, *The Needle, the Pill, and the Saviour* (1966); Vic Ramsey, *The Truth About Drug Addiction* (1966), etc.

CHAPTER 8

1. Jim Griffin, *Gandalf's Garden*, 3 (1968), 12

2. Advertisement for "Flipside", issued by British Youth for Christ, in *Church of England Newspaper*, 15 August 1969

3. Caroline Coon, "The Hippy and the Psychedelic Scene: The Underground Movement", MS. 1969, 2
4. Geoffrey Ostergaard, *Freedom*, 27 August 1960
5. See Jack Kerouac, *On the Road* (1962) and *The Dharma Bums* (1962)
6. See "Aleister Crowley Revisted", *Gandalf's Garden*, 3 (1968), 27–9
7. P. G. Stafford and B. H. Golightly, *LSD: The Problem-Solving Psychedelic* (1967), 156
8. Jim Griffin, op. cit.
9. *I.T.* 1–14 August 1969, 9
10. *Gandalf's Garden*, 1 (1968), 27
11. Ibid. 5 (1969), 2
12. Ibid. 4
13. Ibid. 9
14. Ibid. 2 (1968), 20
15. Timothy Leary, Ralph Metzner, and Richard Alpert, *The Psychedelic Experience* (1966), 11
16. Colin MacInnes, *New Society*, 2 March 1967
17. Alasdair MacIntyre, *New Society*, 6 April 1967
18. D. X. Freedom, *Archives of General Psychiatry* 18 (1968), 345
19. Glin Bennet, *Brit. J. Psych.* 114 (1968), 1222
20. William James, *The Varieties of Religious Experience* (1902), 388
21. Allan Y. Cohen, *New Society*, 11 August 1966, 226–8
22. Wilson Van Dusen, *Psychologia*, 4 (1961), 11–16
23. Alan W. Watts, *This is It* (1960), 17
24. Alan W. Watts, *The Joyous Cosmology* (1962), 17
25. Timothy Leary, Richard Alpert, and Ralph Metzner in R. Blum (ed.), *Utopiates* (1964), 179
26. Timothy Leary in *The Psychedelic Reader* (ed. Weil, Metzner, and Leary) (1965), 195–6
27. League of Spiritual Discovery. MS.
28. Timothy Leary in *Running Man*, 1 (undated), 14
29. Richard Alpert in R. Alpert and S. Cohen *LSD* (1966), 60
30. See Walter Pahnke in R. C. DeBold and R. C. Leaf (ed.), *LSD, Man, and Society* (1969), 60–84; C. A. Weber, S.J. "Religious Aspects", MS. 1967
31. R. E. L. Masters and Jean Houston, *The Varieties of Psychedelic Experience* (1966), 313
32. Frank Lake, *Clinical Theology* (1966), xxii
33. R. C. Zaehner, *Mysticism Sacred and Profane* (1961), 12
34. Allan Y. Cohen, *The A.R.E. Journal*, 3:4 (1968), 31
35. *God in a Pill? Meher Baba on LSD and the High Roads* (1966), 1
36. Ibid., 2
37. Ibid., 2

38. Ibid., 3
39. Allan Y. Cohen, *Boston Globe Sunday Magazine*, 7 August 1966
40. Allan Y. Cohen, "LSD and the Student: approaches to educational strategies", MS. 1967, 15
41. "Blessings in Shades of Green", *The Times*, 15 July 1967
42. *The Cloud of Unknowing* (trans. C. Wolters, 1961), 106, 114
43. *Complete Works of St John of the Cross* (ed. E. Alison Peers, 1947), Volume 1, *Ascent*, Bk. 2, ch. 11, para. 3
44. Anthony Bloom, *Asceticism: (Somatopsychic Techniques)* (1957), 9
45. Ibid., 24
46. Two interesting papers, both American, are Lisa Bieberman, *Phanerothyme, a Western Approach to the Religious use of Psychochemicals* (1968) and Joseph Havens, "A Memo to Quakers on the consciousness-expanding drugs", MS. 1963
47. *Organization and Co-ordination of Federal Drug Research and Regulatory Programs: LSD. Hearings before the Sub-committee on Executive Re-organization of the Committee on Government Operations. U.S. Senate 89th Congress.* 24–26 May 1966, 158–62
48. *Gandalf's Garden*, 2 (1968), 20
49. R. D. Laing in *The Role of Religion in Mental Health* (1967), 51–8
50. On *The Velvet Underground*, LP.
51. William Burroughs, *Guardian*, 7 July 1969

CHAPTER 9

1. Frank Lake, *Clinical Theology* (1966), xxvi
2. Ulrich Simon, *A Theology of Auschwitz* (1967), 124
3. Michael Fordham, *Psychiatry: Its Definition and its Practice* (1967), 21
4. Teilhard de Chardin, *Le Milieu Divin* (1957), 88
5. Stanley G. Evans, *The Church in the Back Streets* (1962), 48
6. R. D. Laing in *The Role of Religion in Mental Health* (1967), 57
7. St John of the Cross, *The Ascent of Mount Carmel*, Prologue, para. 4 in E. Alison Peers (ed.) *Complete Works of St John of the Cross* (1947), I.13
8. *Ascent*, I.2, para. 5, in ibid., I.21
9. Simon, op. cit., 127
10. Eric Hayman, *Disciplines of the Spiritual Life* (1957) 58
11. Thomas Merton, *The Sign of Jonas* (1953), 41
12. John A. T. Robinson, *On Being the Church in the World* (1964), 71
13. Jan Van Ruysbroeck, *The Seven Steps of the Ladder of Spiritual Love*, 7 (trans. F. Sherwood Taylor, 1944 ed., 57, 63)

Some Useful Addresses

1. OFFICIAL BODIES

Home Office Drugs Branch, Romney House, Marsham Street, London, S.W.1. (799–3488).

Department of Health, Alexander Fleming House, Elephant and Castle, London, S.E.1. (407–5522).

The Home office deals with notifications of addicts under the Dangerous Drugs Regulations. The Department of Health deals with questions of treatment.

2. TREATMENT CENTRES FOR DRUG DEPENDENCE

There are drug dependence clinics in London at the following hospitals:

Drug Addiction Clinic, Norwood and District Hospital, Hermitage Road, S.E.19. (653–1171.)

Psychiatric Annexe, Charing Cross Hospital, 1a, Bedfordbury, W.C.2. (836–6835.)

Special Psychiatric Unit, Hackney Hospital, E.9. (985–5555.)

Drug Dependence Clinic, Lambeth Hospital, Brook Drive, S.E.11. (735–6155.)

Addiction Treatment and Research Unit, Maudsley Hospital, 101, Denmark Hill, S.E.5. (703–5411.)

Drug Dependence Centre, St Mary's Hospital, Woodfield Road, W.9. (286–7371.)

Drug Treatment Centre, Queen Mary's Hospital, Roehampton Lane, S.W.15. (788–7211.)

Addiction Unit, St Clement's Hospital, 2a, Bow Road, E.3. (980–4899.)

Drug Dependence Treatment Unit, Day Hospital, St George's Hospital, Tooting Grove, S.W.17. (672–1255.)

Drug Addiction Unit, St Giles' Centre, Camberwell Church Street, S.E.5. (703–5841.)

Simmons House, St Luke's (Woodside) Hospital, Woodside Avenue, N.10. (883–8498.)

Drug Addiction Centre, University College Hospital, Gower Street, W.C.1. (935–6633.)

Drug Addiction Centre, Psychiatric Department, West Middlesex Hospital, Isleworth, Middlesex (560–2121.)

Treatment Centre, Westminster Hospital, 52, Vincent Square, S.W.1. (828–9811.)

Details of clinics and facilities in the rest of the country can be obtained from the Regional Hospital Boards:

Newcastle Regional Hospital Board, Benfield Road, Walker Gate, Newcastle-upon-Tyne 6.

Birmingham Regional Hospital Board, Arthur Thomson House, 146–150, Hagley Road, Birmingham 16.

Sheffield Regional Hospital Board, Fulwood House, Old Fulwood Road, Sheffield S103TH.

Manchester Regional Hospital Board, Gateway House, Piccadilly South, Manchester 1 M66 7LP.

Wessex Regional Hospital Board, Highcroft, Romsey Road, Winchester, Hants.

Oxford Regional Hospital Board, Old Road, Headington, Oxford.

Leeds Regional Hospital Board, Park Parade, Harrogate, Yorkshire.

East Anglian Regional Hospital Board, Union Lane, Chesterton, Cambridge.

Liverpool Regional Hospital Board, Wilberforce House, The Strand, Liverpool 2.

South Western Regional Hospital Board, 27, Tyndalls Park Road, Bristol 8.

Welsh Office, Cathays Park, Cardiff.

N.W., N.E., S.E. and S.W. Regional Boards, 40 Eastbourne Terrace, London, W.2.

3. RESEARCH BODIES

Addiction Research Unit, Institute of Psychiatry, 101, Denmark Hill, London, S.E.5. (703–5411.)

Institute for the Study of Drug Dependence, Chandos House, 2, Queen Anne Street, London, W.1. (580–2518.)

National Addiction and Research Institute, 88, Beaufort Street, London, S.W.3. (352–9330.) (This centre, although not one of the official drug dependence clinics, has probably the only clinic where the Dole-Nyswander "methadone maintenance" programme is operated in a way similar to that in the U.S.A.)

4. GROUPS CONCERNED WITH WELFARE AND SOCIAL ACTION

Association for Prevention of Addiction, c/o Gilston House, Near Harlow, Essex.

Life for the World, Northwick Park, Blockley, Moreton-in-the-Marsh, Gloucestershire. (0386–76–440.)

Release, 50a, Princedale Road, London, W.11. (Legal advice for those arrested on drugs charges.) Office: 229–7753. 24-Hour Service: 603–8654.

Rink Club (Salvation Army), Regent Hall, 275, Oxford Street, London, W.1. (629–5424.)

St Anne's House, 57, Dean Street, Soho, London, W.1. (437–5006.)

St Martin-in-the-Field's Social Service Unit, 5, St Martin's Place, London, W.C.2. 24-Hour Telephone: 930–1732.

Simon Community, 129, Malden Road, London, N.W.5. (485–6639.)

Select Bibliography

The literature on drug use is enormous. This is only a very select list of books and articles. A fuller bibliography may be obtained from the author, St Anne's House, 57, Dean Street, London, W.1.

GENERAL

Bewley, T. H., "Recent changes in the pattern of drug abuse in the U.K.", *Bull. Narc.* 18:4 (1966), 1–13.

Birdwood, George, *The Willing Victim; A Parent's Guide to Drug Abuse.* Secker and Warburg 1969.

Dawtry, Frank, ed., *Social Problems of Drug Abuse: A Guide for Social Workers.* Butterworth 1968.

Eddy, Nathan B., Halbach, H., Isbell, H., and Seevers. M. H., "Drug dependence: its significance and characteristics", *Bull. W.H.O.* 32:5 (1965), 721–33.

Glatt, M. M., Pittman, D. J., Gillespie, D. G., and Hills, D. R., *The Drug Scene in Great Britain.* Edward Arnold 1967.

Graham, J. D. P., *Pharmacology for Medical Students.* Oxford University Press 1966.

Harms, Ernest, ed., *Drug Addiction in Youth.* Pergamon 1964.

Hollander, Charles, ed., *Background Papers on Student Drug Involvement.* Washington, U.S. National Student Association 1967.

Joyce, C. R. B., ed., *Psychopharmacology: Dimensions and Perspectives.* Tavistock 1968.

Laurie, Peter, *Drugs: Medical, Psychological and Social Facts.* Penguin 1967.

Leech, Kenneth, *The Drug Subculture.* Church Information Office 1969.

Leech, Kenneth, and Jordan, Brenda, *Drugs for Young People: Their Use and Misuse.* Religious Education Press 1967.

Lingeman, Richard R., *Drugs from A to Z: A Dictionary*. New York, McGraw-Hill 1969.

Louria, D. M., *Nightmare Drugs*. New York, Pocket Books 1966.

Mitchell, A. R. K., *Drugs: The Parent's Dilemma*. Royston, Priory Press, 1969.

Silberman, Martin, *Aspects of Drug Addiction*. Royal London Prisoners' Aid Society 1967.

Steinberg, Hannah, ed., *The Scientific Basis of Drug Dependence*. J. and A. Churchill 1969.

Todd, G. R., ed., *Extra Pharmacopoeia: Martindale*. Pharmaceutical Press, 1967 ed.

Willis, J. H., *Drug Dependence: A Study for Nurses and Social Workers*. Faber 1969.

Wilson, C. W. M., ed., *The Pharmacological and Epidemiological Aspects of Adolescent Drug Dependence*. Pergamon 1968.

Wood, Anthony, *Drug Dependence*. Bristol Health Department 1967.

AMPHETAMINES, BARBITURATES, ETC.

Connell, P. H., "Amphetamine Misuse", *Brit. J. Add.* 60 (1964), 9–27.

Connell, P. H., *Amphetamine Psychosis*. Institute of Psychiatry, Chapman and Hall 1958.

Connell, P. H., "The use and abuse of amphetamines", *Practitioner* 200 (1968), 234–43.

Cooper, Peter, *Poisoning by Drugs and Chemicals*. Alchemist Publications 1958.

Glatt, M. M., "The abuse of barbiturates in the U.K.", *Bull. Narc.* 14 : 2 (1962), 19–38.

Hawks, David, Mitcheson, Martin, Ogborne, Alan, and Edwards, Griffith, "The abuse of methylamphetamine", *B.M.J.* 27 July 1969, 715–21.

Kalant, O. J., *The Amphetamines: Toxicity and Addiction*. University of Toronto Press 1966.

Lawson, A. A. H., and Brown, S. S., "Acute methaqualone (Mandrax) poisoning" *Scot. Med. J.* 12 (1967), 63–8.

Mathew, Henry, and Lawson, A. A. H., *Treatment of Common Acute Poisonings*. E. and S. Livingstone 1967.

Morimoto, K., "The problem of the abuse of amphetamines in Japan", *Bull. Narc.* 9:3 (1957), 8–12.

Ogborne, Alan, "The methedrine scene", *New Society*, 26 June 1969.

Oswald, Ian, and Thacore, V. R., "Amphetamine and phenmetrazine addiction", *B.M.J.* 17 August 1963, 427–31.

Scott, P. D., and Wilcox, D. R. C., "Delinquency and the amphetamines", *Brit. J. Add.* 61 (1965), 9–27.

HEROIN

de Alarcon, R., "The spread of heroin abuse in a community", *Bull. Narc.* 21:3 (1969), 17–22.

de Alarcon, R., and Rathod, N. H., "Prevalance and early detection of heroin abuse", *B.M.J.* 1 June 1968, 549–53.

Bewley, T. H., "The diagnosis and management of heroin addiction", *Practitioner*, 200 (1968), 215–19.

Bewley, T. H., "Heroin addiction in the U.K. (1954–1964)", *B.M.J.* 27 November 1965, 1284–6.

Chein, Isidor, Gerard, Donald L., Lee, Robert S., and Rosenfeld, Eva, *Narcotics, Delinquency and Social Policy: The Road to H.* Tavistock 1964.

D'Orban, P. T., "Heroin dependence and delinquency in women —a study of heroin addicts in Holloway Prison", MS. 1969 (in the press).

Drug Addiction. 2nd Report of the Interdepartmental Committee. H.M.S.O. 1965.

Eddy, Nathan B., "The chemotherapy of drug dependence", *Brit. J. Add.* 61 (1966), 155–67.

Edwards, Griffith, "The British approach to the treament of heroin addiction", *Lancet*, 12 April 1969, 768–72.

Edwards, Griffith, "The relevance of American experience of narcotic addiction to the British scene", *B.M.J.* 12 August 1967, 425–9.

James, I. P., "Delinquency and heroin addiction in Britain", *Brit. J. Crim.* April 1969, 108–24.

James, I. P., "Suicide and mortality amongst heroin addicts in Britain", *Brit. J. Add.* 62 (1967), 391–8.

Larner, Jeremy, and Tefferteller, Ralph, *The Addict in the Street.* Penguin 1966.

Lindesmith, Alfred R., *Opiate Addiction*. Chicago, Aldine 1968 ed.

Rathod, N. H., de Alarcon, R., and Thomson, I. G., "Signs of heroin usage detected by drug users and their parents", *Lancet*, 30 December 1967, 1411–14.

Schur, E. M., *Narcotic Addiction in Britain and America*. Tavistock 1963.

Wikler, Abraham, *Opiate Addiction*. Springfield, Illinois, Charles C. Thomas 1953.

Wilner, D. M., and Kassebaum, G. G., *Narcotics*. New York, McGraw-Hill 1965.

CANNABIS

Allentuck, S., and Bowman, K. M., "The psychiatric aspects of marihuana intoxication", *Am. J. Psych.* 99 (1942), 248–51.

Andrews, George, and Vinkenoog, Simon, *The Book of Grass*. Peter Owen 1967.

Bloomquist, E. R., *Marijuana*. Beverley Hills, Glencoe Press 1968.

Cannabis. A report by the Advisory Committee on Drug Dependence. H.M.S.O. 1969.

Glatt, M. M., "Is it all right to smoke pot?", *Brit. J. Add.* 64 (1969), 109–14.

Goode, Erich, ed., *Marijuana*. New York, Atherton Press 1969.

Isbell, H., *et alia*, "Effects of (−) Δ^9-trans-tetrahydrocannabinol in man", *Psychopharmacologia*, 11 (1967), 184–8.

Leonard, B. E., "Cannabis: a short review of its effects and possible dangers of its use", *Brit. J. Add.* 64 (1969), 121–30.

Murphy, H. B., "The cannabis habit", *Bull. Narc.* 15 (1963), 15–23.

Report of the Indian Hemp Drugs Commission 1893–4. Simla, Government Printing Office, 7 Volumes, 1897.

Rosevear, John, *Pot. A Handbook of Marijuana*. New York, University Books 1967.

Solomon, David, ed., *The Marihuana Papers*. New American Library 1966. British edition, Panther Books 1969.

Weil, A. T., Zinberg, N. T., and Nelson, J. M., "Clinical and psychological effects of marihuana in man", *Science* 162 (1968), 1234–42.

Wolstenholme, G. E. W., and Knight, Julie, ed., *Hashish: its Chemistry and Pharmacology*. J. and A. Churchill 1965.

Zinberg, Norman, and Weil, Andrew, "Cannabis: the first controlled experiment", *New Society*, 16 January 1969.

LSD

Alpert, Richard, and Cohen, Sidney, *LSD*. New American Library 1966.

Blum, Richard H., *et al.*, *Utopiates*. Tavistock 1965.

Cohen, Allan Y., "Who takes LSD and why?", *New Society*, 11 August 1966.

Cohen, Sidney, *Drugs of Hallucination*. Secker and Warburg 1964.

Cohen, Sidney, "Psychotomimetic Agents", *Annual Review of Pharmacology*, 7 (1967), 301–18.

Crocket, Richard, Sandison, R. A., and Walk, Alexander, *Hallucinogenic Drugs and their Psychotherapeutic Use*. H. K. Lewis and Co. 1963.

DeBold, R. C., and Leaf, R. C., ed., *LSD, Man and Society*. Faber 1969.

Hoffer, A., and Osmond, H., *The Hallucinogens*. New York, Academy Press, 1967.

Joyce, C. R. B., "Psychedelics" in Rose, Stephen, ed., *Chemical and Biological Warfare*. Harrap 1968, 35–43.

Masters, R. E. L., and Houston, Jean, *The Varieties of Psychedelic Experience*. New York, Delta Books 1966.

Rinkel, Max, and Denber, Herman C. B., *Chemical Concepts of Psychosis*. New York, McDowell, Obolensky 1958.

Solomon, David, ed., *LSD: The Consciousness-Expanding Drug*. Berkeley, G. P. Putnam's Sons 1967.

Stafford, P. G., and Golightly, B. H., *LSD: The Problem-Solving Psychedelic*. Tandem 1967.

Weil, G. M., Metzner, Ralph, and Leary, Timothy, ed., *The Psychedelic Reader*. New York, University Books 1965.

Wolfe, Tom, *The Electric Kool-Aid Acid Test*. Weidenfeld and Nicholson 1969.

SOCIOLOGICAL

Binnie, H. L., *The Attitudes to Drugs and Drug Takers of Students at the University and Colleges of Higher Education in an English Midland City*. Leicester 1969.

Blenheim Project: Detached Social Work with Young Drifters in London. 2nd Annual Report, 1966.

Burroughs, William, *The Naked Lunch*. Corgi 1968.

Coon, Caroline, and Harris, Rufus, *The Release Report on Drug Offenders and the Law*. Sphere 1969.

Downes, David M., *The Delinquent Solution*. Routledge 1966.

Farquharson, Robin, *Drop Out!* Anthony Blond 1968.

Fyvel, T. R., *The Insecure Offenders*, Penguin 1963.

Lipton, Lawrence, *The Holy Barbarians*. New English Library 1962.

The Portobello Project: Detached Youth Work in West London. Annual Report, 1967.

The Soho Project Report 1967–8. London 1969.

Timms, Noel, *Rootless in the City*. Bedford Square Press, 1969.

Trench, Sally, *Bury Me In My Boots*. Hodder 1968.

West, D. J., *Homosexuality*. Penguin 1968 ed.

PASTORAL CARE

Croft, George, S. J., "Pastoral Counselling" in *The Role of Religion in Mental Health*. National Association of Mental Health 1967, 29–39.

Evans, Stanley G., *The Church in the Back Streets*. Mowbrays 1962.

Halmos, Paul, *The Faith of the Counsellors*. Constable 1965.

Kenrick, Bruce, *Come Out The Wilderness*. Fontana 1965.

Kyle, W. H., ed., *Healing Through Counselling*. Epworth Press 1964.

Kyle, W. H., *The Impact of Psychology on Pastoral Work*. Guild of Pastoral Psychology 1965.

Kyle, W. H., *The Uniqueness of Pastoral Psychotherapy*. Guild of Pastoral Psychology 1969.

Lake, Frank, *Clinical Theology*. Darton, Longman and Todd 1966.

Lambourne, R. A., *Community, Church, and Healing*. Darton, Longman and Todd 1963.

Matthews, Gordon, "Philosophy, methods and aims of the Simon Community", *Case Conference*, 15 (1969), 356–60.

The Rink Report 1968–1969. Salvation Army Rink Club, 1969.

Robinson, John A. T., *On Being the Church in the World*. SCM Press 1964.

SPIRITUALITY

Baba, Meher, *Discourses*. India, Adi K. Irani 1955.

Baba, Meher, *Gems from the Discourses of Meher Baba*. New York, Circle Productions 1945.

Baba, Meher, *God in a Pill? Meher Baba on LSD and the High Roads*. Sufism Reorientated, San Francisco 1966.

Baba, Meher, *Sparks from Meher Baba*. Friends of Meher Baba 1967.

Biebermann, Lisa, *Phanerothyme: A Western Approach to the Religious Use of Psycho-chemicals*. Cambridge, Mass. Psychedelic Information Center 1968.

Bloom, Anthony, *Asceticism (Somatopysychic Techniques)* Guild of Pastoral Psychology 1957.

Bloom, Anthony, *Living Prayer*. Darton, Longman and Todd 1966.

Bouyer, Louis, *Introduction to Spirituality*. Darton, Longman and Todd 1963.

Braden, William, *The Private Sea: LSD and the Search for God*. New York, Bantam Books 1968.

Bryant, Christopher, S.S.J.E., *Prayer and Psychology*. Privately published, N.D.

Cohen, Allan, Y., "God and LSD: the psychedelic illusion", *Boston Globe Sunday Magazine*, 7 August 1966.

Cohen, Allan Y., "The journey beyond trips" *The A.R.E. Journal*, 3:4 (1968), 26–33.

Dechanet, J-M., O.S.B., *Christian Yoga*. Burns Oates 1964.

Enomiya-Lassalle, H. M., S.J., "Enlightenment serving the Christian ascetic and mystic" in *Zen-Way to Enlightenment*. Burns Oates 1967.

Fordham, Michael, "The Dark Night of the Soul" in *The Objective Psyche*. Routledge 1958, 130–48.

Gandalf's Garden. London 1968 onwards.

Griffiths, Bede, O.S.B., *Christian Ashram: Essays towards a Hindu-Christian Dialogue*. Darton, Longman and Todd 1966.

Huxley, Aldous, *The Doors of Perception* and *Heaven and Hell*. Penguin 1965.

James, William, *The Varieties of Religious Experience*. Longmans 1902.

Jung, C. G., *Psychology and Religion East and West*. Routledge 1958.

Laing, R. D., "Religious experience and the role of organized religion" in *The Role of Religion in Mental Health*. National Association for Mental Health 1967, 51–8.

Leary, Timothy, *Psychedelic Prayers after the Tao Te Ching*. New York, Poets Press 1966.

Leary, Timothy, "The religious experience: its production and interpretation" in Weil, Metzner and Leary (ed.) *The Psychedelic Reader*. New York, University Books 1965, 191–213.

Leary, Timothy, Metzner, Ralph, and Alpert, Richard, *The Psychedelic Experience*. New York, University Books 1965.

Merton, Thomas, *Mystics and Zen Masters*. New York, Farrar, Straus and Giroux 1967.

Peers, E. Alison, ed., *The Complete Works of St John of the Cross*. Burns Oates 1947. Volume 1.

Rhymes, Douglas, *Prayer in the Secular City*. Lutterworth 1967.

van Ruysbroeck, Jan, *The Seven Steps of the Ladder of Spiritual Love*. Dacre ed. 1944.

Sophrony, Archimandrite, *Principles of Orthodox Asceticism*. Oxford, Holywell Press 1964.

Thornton, Martin, *The Rock and the River*. Hodder 1965.

Underhill, Evelyn, *Mysticism*. Methuen 1940.

Zaehner, R. C., *Mysticism Sacred and Profane*. Oxford University Press 1961.

PRIESTHOOD

Leech, Kenneth, "The drug subculture and the role of the priest", *Ministry*, Spring, 1969, 19–26.

Simon, Ulrich, *A Theology of Auschwitz*. Gollancz 1967.

Thornton, Martin, "The Anglican tradition of priesthood" in *Essays in Pastoral Reconstruction*. SPCK 1960, 35-47.

Index

Aaku, Joseph 38
abstinence syndrome 6, 7, 11, 31f, 35
Adams, G. B. 10
addiction 6–7, 9, 16, 21–36
alcohol 5, 11, 18, 20, 33, 44, 64
Aldermaston March 39, 62
Allentuck and Bowman 44
Alles 13
Alpert, Richard 49, 102
amitriptylene 5
amphetamines 11, 12, 13–20, 33, 47, 48, 64, 65–8, 69, 71f, 86, 89
amylobarbitone 5, 10, 13, 15, 18
Amytal 10, 11
anaesthesia 16
Andrade, O. M. 44
anointing 126
antibiotics 43
antidepressants 5, 12, 41
antihistamines 19
Anti-University 101
Arts Lab 101
Asuni, T. 43
aversion therapy 35

Baba, Meher 107–8
"bad trips" 88f
Baez, Joan 62
Banton, M. P. 38
barbitone 5
barbiturates 4, 5, 6, 7, 9–12, 18f, 26
Bayer, Alfred 5
Beatles, The 49, 78
beatniks 39, 42, 59, 69f
Becker, H. S. 44

Benabud, A. 43
Benzedrine 13, 14
benzodiazepines 5
Bevan, Geoff 83
Bewley, T. H. 39
bhang 37
BIT 101
Biven, Barrie 83
Blood, Benjamin 103
Bloom, Anthony 110f
"blues" 13
Boots 19
brain 4, 17, 52
Brain Report 1961 21
Brain Report 1965 24–5, 65, 66
Brazil 44
Brietal 10
British Medical Association 15
British Pharmaceutical Codex 43
"British system" 9
Bruce, Lenny 59
Buddha 7, 99
Buddhism 98–9
bufotenine 53
Burroughs, William 30, 42
butobarbitone 10
Byrds, The 78

California 53
Campaign for Nuclear Disarmament 62, 70
cannabidiol 42
cannabinol 42
cannabis 5, 37–48, 59–65, 69, 71f, 79, 85f
Cardiff 60
Casablanca 44

central nervous system 3
charas 37
Chein, I. 33, 73
Chinese heroin 26
chloral hydrate 9
chlordiazepoxide 5
chlorpromazine 5, 20, 54
Chopras 43f
Cloud of Unknowing, The 110
coca 8
cocaine 8, 14
codeine 8, 19
Cohen, Allan Y. 53, 103f, 107f, 112
Cohen, Sidney 51
Coke Hole Trust 92
Commune of the Streets 70
confession 124f
Connell, P. H. 15, 16
Coon, Caroline 76, 98
cough mixtures 8
Crawley 27-8
crime 34f
Cross and the Switchblade, The 93
Crowley, Aleister 98
cyclazocine 35
Cyprus 39

dagga 37
Dangerous Drugs Acts 9, 23, 25, 74
Daprisal 15
Daytop 36
Departmental Committee on Morphine and Heroin Addiction 9
depersonalization 52
depression 16
Desbutal 15
dexamphetamine 13, 14ff, 67, 73
Dexedrine, see dexamphetamine
Dexten 15
Dexytal 15
diazepam 5
Diesed 15

Diggers 101
dimethyltriptamine 53
Dole and Nyswander 35, 74f
DOM 54
Donovan 62
D'Orban, P. T. 34, 35, 48, 67-8, 74
Doriden 11, 19
Dover's Powder 8
Downes, David 61-2
drifters 71f
Drinamyl 11, 13f, 67, 73
drug abuse 5, 6
drug action 3-4
drug dependence 6-7, 16, 30-6
drug misuse 5, 6
Durophet 15, 19, 67
Dylan, Bob 59, 62, 78

East Harlem Protestant Parish 90
Edeleano 13
Edinburgh Poisoning Centre 20
Ellis, Havelock 50
enuresis 16
epilepsy 10, 16
ergot 50
Erlenmeyer 8
escalation 46-8
esrar 37
euphoria 8, 41
Evans, Stanley 119
exorcism 127
Ezekiel 38

Ferlinghetti, Lawrence 59
folk music 42, 62f
Fugs, The 78

Gambia 61
Gandalf's Garden 100-2
ganga 37
Geneva Convention 39
Ginsberg, Allan 59
Glass, Ruth 69
Glatt, M. M. 33, 37, 42

glutethimide 11, 18
Goode, Erich 47, 63
Griffin, Jim 97

habituation 6
Hague Opium Convention 8
Haight-Ashbury 108
Haley, Bill 62
hallucinations 16, 51, 52
Hao-Tho 38
Harrison Act 9
hashish, see cannabis
Hawks, D. et alia 68
Herodotus 8
heroin 5, 9, 18, 21–36, 46, 48, 63f,
    71f, 73–5, 86f, 113–15
Hesiod 7
hexobarbitone 10
Highgate Counselling Centre 91
Hinduism 98ff, 104
hippies 42, 64, 75–9, 97f
Hippocrates 8
Hofmann, A. 50
Home Office 24
homosexuality 33f, 68
Hong Kong 26
Hoxton 83
Huxley, Aldous 49, 103
5-hydroxytriptamine 5
hypnotics 9–12, 18–20
hypodermic 8
hypothalamus 14

I Ching 112
imipramine 5
immigrants 39, 46, 60, 62
Incredible String Band 78
India 43
Indian Hemp Commission 40, 44
insomnia 10
intercession 123
International Times 79
Isbell, H. 42, 45
Itkin, M. F. 111

James, I. P. 35
James, William 103f
Jansch, Bert 114
Japan 13–14
jazz 42, 60
Jethro Tull 78
John of the Cross, St 110, 122
Johnson, D. McL. 38
Jones, John 3, 8
Joyce, C. R. B. 46
"junkies' doctors" 24–5

Kerouac, Jack 49, 98
kif 37
Kirkpatrick, W. J. 33
Kolb, L. 33
Krishna Consciousness 98

Laing, R. D. 112
Lake, Frank 106, 117
Largactil 5, 54
laudanum 8
Laudenheimer, R. 10
League for Spiritual Discovery 105
Leary, Timothy 49, 52, 53, 54,
    102, 104f, 108f
Lebanon 39, 41
Levinstein 8
Lewis, Sir Aubrey 44
Librium 5
Life for the World 92
Lindesmith, A. R. 32
Lipton, Lawrence 59f
Liverpool 38, 60
Lord of the Rings 100
Louria, D. M. 51
lysergic acid diethylamide (LSD)
    4, 47, 49–55, 63, 69, 79, 89, 99,
    102–113, 122

MacInnes, Colin 102
McCarthy, Paddy 83
Mafia 25
Magna Carta 78
Ma-Lo 38
Manchester 60

Mandrax, see methaqualone
Marie de la Trinité 116
marijuana, see cannabis
Masters and Houston 106
May and Baker 5
Melsed, Melsedin 11, 19
mephentermine 15
Mephine 15
meprobamate 5
Merton, Thomas 123
mescaline 49, 54
methadone 18, 19, 26, 31, 35, 74–5
methaqualone 11, 19–20
Methedrine, see methylampheta-
    mine
methylamphetamine 13–18, 35, 48,
    50, 67f, 72f
methylphenidate 15, 16, 17
methylprylone 11
Metzner, Ralph 49, 102
Mexico 49
Middle Earth 79, 101
Ministry of Health 13, 17
Mogadon 5, 11
Morocco 43
morphine 5, 6, 8, 9, 21
mysticism 102–13

narcolepsy 13, 15, 16
Nebuchadnezzar 38
Nembutal 10, 11
New York 28–30, 47, 51, 60, 93
New York Mayor's Committee 40
Niemann, Albert 8
Nigeria 43, 61
nitrazepam 5, 11
nitrous oxide 102
Nodular 11
nor-adrenalin 4–5
Notting Hill 63, 83

obesity 16
Ogata 13
opiates 5, 7, 9, 21–36, 46, 86
opium 3, 5, 7–8

Osmond, Humphrey 49
overdose 88f

Pakistan 39
paraldehyde 9
paranoia 16, 41, 51
pastoral care 80–96
Pentangle, The 78
pentobarbitone 5, 10, 11, 15
Pentothal 10
Persia 38
Pervitin 13
pethidine 9
pharmacognosy 4
pharmacology 4
pharmacy 4
phenmetrazine 14, 15, 18, 67
phenobarbitone 5, 10
phenothiazines 6, 11, 54
phentermine 15
Phoenix Houses 36
Physeptone, see methadone
Piccadilly 70, 74–5
"pillhead" 17
poisoning 89
pop music 42
"pot", see cannabis
Powick Hospital 50
Pravaz 8
Preludin, see phenmetrazine
priesthood 116–26
psilocybin 53
psychedelic 5, 49, 52, 53, 64, 97,
    102–13
psychopathy 16, 33f
psychosis 13–17, 39, 43–5, 50–5
psychotomimetic 5, 39, 50f
Puerto Ricans 29
"purple hearts" 13

quinalbarbitone 5, 10, 18
Quintessence 100

Ramirez 36, 83
Release 76, 92, 101

Riker 19
Rink Club 84, 90
Ritalin 15
Robinson, J. A. T. 123–4
rock n' roll 62
Rolleston Committee 9

sacraments 123–6
salvation 80f
Salvation Army 71, 84–90
Sandison, R. A. 50, 52
Scandinavia 54
schizophrenia 16, 50
Schur, E. M., 61
Secret of the Golden Flower, The 112
sedatives 5, 9–12, 18–20
serotonin 4–5, 53
sexual disturbances 33–4
Shanghai Opium Convention 8
Sierra Leone 61
Simon Community 84f
Simon, Paul 62, 63, 78
Simon, Ulrich 122
Single Convention 39
Smith, Kline, and French 13
Soho 14, 26, 38, 48, 65ff, 73, 82, 83
Soma Research Association 42
Somalia 61
Soneryl 10, 11
South Africa 44
Spelthorne St Mary 92
spirituality 53, 97–115, 120–3
Stepney 38, 60f, 73–4
stereotactic surgery 35
Stewart, Al 62
stimulants 5
STP 54
students 69
strychnine 26
subculture 47f, 61f
Suzuki, D. T. 98
Sweden 14, 18
Sydenham, Thomas 8
sympathomimetic 14

Synanon 36
synapses 4

takrouri 37
Tao Te Ching 112
Teilhard de Chardin 118
tetrahydrocannabinol 42, 45
therapeutic addicts 9–12
thiopentone 10
Tibetan Book of the Dead 109
TMA 54
Tofranil 5
Tolkien, J. R. 100
tranquillizers 5, 6, 11, 12, 19
Trench, Sally 69–70
Tryptizol 5
Tuinal 18
Tylden, Elizabeth 43, 45
Tyrannosaurus Rex 78, 100

Underground 70, 75–9, 97–102, 121–2
Underhill, Evelyn 104
United Nations 9, 24
United States 28–30, 35, 47, 49, 51, 59, 61–2, 63f, 67, 74, 93, 107

Valium 5
Veronal 9

Ward, Barbara 83
Ward, Stephen 38
Watts, Alan 98, 104
Wikler, A. 32
Wilkerson, David 93
Willis, J. H. 33
Wootton Report 40, 44, 47
World Health Organization 4, 6, 7

Young and Scoville 14

Zaehner, R. C. 107
Zen 60, 98–9, 104
Zend Avesta 38
Zinberg, N. T. 41